PICTURE IT
IN
MACHINE APPLIQUÉ

PICTURE IT
IN
MACHINE APPLIQUÉ

SUE SIMMONS

David & Charles

(above) Sunny Window Wallhanging, (previous page) Fresh Flowers Wallhanging, Flowers for You Cushion, Simply Floral Cushion and Happy Hearts Wallhangings

A DAVID & CHARLES BOOK

Copyright text, designs and illustrations © Sue Simmons 1994

Photography © David & Charles 1994

First published 1994

Sue Simmons has asserted her right to be identified as author of this work in accordance with the Copyright, Designs and Patents Act 1988.

A catalogue record for this book is available from the British Library.

ISBN 0 7153 0034 2

Typeset by ICON Graphic Services, Exeter
and printed in England by Butler & Tanner Ltd, Frome
for David & Charles
Brunel House   Newton Abbot   Devon

CONTENTS

INTRODUCTION

This book has been planned and written as a basic guide to machine appliqué for those who have never tried it before (and for those who have – new inspiration is always exciting and valuable). A basic knowledge of sewing and a swing needle (zig-zag) sewing machine are the only essentials required.

Colour, design, fabrics, preparation and stitching are covered in a very simple straightforward manner. The projects progress from very easy at the beginning through to more adventurous, but all can be tackled by a beginner, and will provide a springboard for designing and making original new projects for yourself.

I began machine appliqué some eighteen years ago, making items for my young children, and I enjoy combining it with embroidery, patchwork and quilting. Over the years, I have developed a love of working with colours and fabrics, and in this book I have explained the methods I have learnt, developed and use. New approaches evolve constantly, and this is part of the endless fascination of this work. The shapes are pared down to childlike simplicity, but retain their essence – I have learnt to look at the world with new eyes and delight in the forms and colours that surround us.

So, this book is an attempt to transmit to you my love of stitching, to stimulate creativity, and awaken an awareness of beauty, colour and form. Above all, I hope you gain enormous pleasure and fulfilment from your stitching.

Work is love made visible.
THE PROPHET KAHIL GIBRAN

(right) Breakfast Time Placemats and Rainy Day Child's Bag

BASIC TECHNIQUES

EQUIPMENT

SEWING MACHINE

As the fabric shapes are applied using satin stitch, your machine must have a swing needle (zig-zag) action and make neat even stitches. Try out your machine before starting a project and learn the satin stitch technique. It is very frustrating to be ready to start then discover that the machine will not stitch in the way you need it to. Usually the stitch width should be set at 4 (see Stitching Techniques on page 20) and the stitch length at ½–1, depending on your machine and stitch preference.

You may like a tight band of stitching around each piece of appliqué, or the stitches to be slightly apart. Practise and see which you prefer. The standard stitching foot is suitable for machine appliqué; an appliqué foot is obtainable, but it is not a necessity when you are beginning. You need several bobbins for working with different coloured threads, and the needles required are size 80(11) and 70(9).

SEWING KIT

Basic sewing equipment including tacking (basting) cotton, stitch ripper, dressmaking and embroidery scissors – the scissors must be sharp.

FABRICS

These are covered in detail on page 14. Start your own fabric collection by saving pieces left over from each project for future work.

INTERFACING

Use ultra soft light iron-on vilene (pellon), ironed onto the reverse side of all appliqué pieces. It prevents shapes fraying when they are cut out, and enables them to be used without a seam allowance.

THREADS

Cotton or synthetic may be used and should match each fabric you are applying.

SOFT PENCIL

For drawing shapes onto the reverse side of fabrics, use a 2 or 3B.

DRAWING KIT

Paper for design drawing and templates, scissors for cutting paper, pencil, rubber and a sheet of paper large enough for a full-size drawing of your design.

SELF-SEALING PLASTIC BAGS

Very useful for storing fabrics, templates and cut-out fabric shapes, to protect them from becoming grubby or lost.

PLANNING A PROJECT

To begin with make something small and simple, like a wallhanging or cushion. Look at the projects featured on pages 30–91 for ideas and either make one of them or adapt a design to suit something else you want to create. Cushions, wallhangings, aprons, bags, children's clothes, table mats and Christmas articles all lend them-selves to machine appliqué.

Whatever you decide to make will affect your choice of fabrics, for example, will it have to match an existing colour scheme or should it be a sturdy, easily washable fabric for a child's item?

If you want to make a very large wallhanging, it may have to be made in several separate blocks, then stitched together to achieve the desired size.

At this stage in planning your project comes the excitement of selecting colours. Are you choosing certain colours because you love them, because they tone with other colours in a room, or because you are making a gift and know the recipient's favourite colours?

For any single project you need to choose a range of colours which complement one another. Although this is a simple enough task if you deal with colours regularly it can be daunting if you don't. To help allay any fears, read through 'I'm No Good With Colour!' (page 12), which will help you select colours that are both appealing and suitable for your projects. One piece of advice though, in order to see true colours in all their beauty, you should look at a fabric in daylight.

Now consider what type of fabric you need. The section on Fabrics (page 14) gives information on what to select and helps you make your choice from the fabulous range available.

Sometimes ideas for designs do not come easily to the beginner, but we are surrounded by wonderful sources. Use the designs in the project section of this book as starting points, they are all graded. Once you have tried a couple of them, you may want to modify the designs or create your own original and unique work.

Other design sources worth looking at include:
♥ Cards – there are many beautiful designs on the market.
♥ Children's books – many have fabulous, colourful yet simple illustrations.
♥ Photographs – Start taking your own photos of objects and views you find pleasing.
♥ Views through windows.
♥ Views through gates.
♥ Gardens – look at flowerpots, flowers, garden shapes, trees.
♥ The countryside – look at old farm gates, trees, the shape of the hills.

·CARDS·

·COLOURS & DESIGNS·

Simplicity is the key, at least whilst learning the techniques, and it shows colour and shape to their best advantage.

You may want to draw your own design, but feel inhibited by your lack of ability. In the section 'But I Can't Draw!' (page 16) there are suggestions to help you overcome this, which will give you the confidence to draw simple shapes successfully.

'I'M NO GOOD WITH COLOUR!'

'I cannot select colours', 'I'm no good with colour', 'I cannot put colours together to make them look right'. Not true! Everyone can become aware of colour.

Once you let go of your fear by experimenting with colour you will discover your own inherent ability to select a range of colours for your work. Try walking through your home collecting all the items you like the colour of. Now sort them out until you have a small group which you think looks particularly good together. Do this several times using different items, so that eventually the task becomes absorbing and easier. These groups of colours can then be used as the basis for your projects. Do remember that colour is very personal – what pleases one person may not please another – and, ultimately, your choice has to satisfy and stimulate you alone.

If you are hesitant and unsure about your colour judgement, you could just copy the colours from a picture you like, using them as the basis for your work, minimizing the number of colours used. As you repeat this process you will gradually find out which colour combinations you like. Eventually, as your confidence grows, you will be able to make your own exciting selections.

There are various ways to become familiar with colour. Study the natural world, nature is an expert at putting colours together in unlikely combinations. Look at autumn leaves, bricks covered with lichen, the flowers found in herbaceous borders. See how colours are put together in illustrated books and magazines, especially those on patchwork, embroidery and knitting. Wander round a wool shop, study the ranges of embroidery threads. Go to an art shop and observe the selections of coloured paints and crayons. Look through the shade cards produced by paint manufacturers. Even a flower shop or a greengrocers has something to teach you about colour, how it can be used and the combinations that go together. Learn to observe and contemplate.

Follow all these suggestions and you will be opening your mind to colour awareness and the beauty of colour. As a bonus, you may also make some observations about the shapes that surround us!

FABRICS

The most suitable fabrics for machine appliqué are 100 per cent natural fibres. Do not mix synthetic and natural fibres, they can behave differently when used and/or washed, jeopardizing the quality of your work.

The chosen fabrics should be compatible with the use of the finished piece. Ask yourself if the item needs to be washable? Does the base fabric need to be tough? Is it to be a cushion with a slightly textured base/background fabric? Take some time thinking about the fabrics before you start choosing, then enjoy collecting them!

BASE FABRIC

This fabric will be used as the base onto which the appliqué pieces are stitched, and may double as the background. The base needs to be firm, to prevent puckering occurring at the stitch lines when you apply your shapes.

Ideally use any close weave medium-weight cotton: calico (muslin), ticking (pillow ticking), Indian Goa, broadcloth, needlecord and towelling are all suitable base fabrics. Try experimenting with different fabrics to discover which ones you like to use. For a small design on a lightweight cotton – a child's dress or a napkin for example – tack (baste) several layers of tissue paper to the reverse side of the fabric, then stitch on the appliqué pieces, when complete, tear away the tissue paper. This prevents the base fabric from puckering, but should only be used for small areas of appliqué. The use of wadding (batting) under a background fabric can give a pleasing quilted effect, and is worth considering.

BACKGROUND FABRICS

These fabrics provide the background to your appliqué and may be one and the same as the base fabric. However, it may be appropriate to your design to use coloured and/or printed lightweight cotton as your background, which may be too lightweight to take the appliqué without puckering. Use calico (muslin) as the base

and cover it with the chosen background cotton, which has vilene (pellon) ironed onto its reverse side. Tack (baste) the background fabric securely to the base calico (muslin) to prevent slipping; you now have a firm base for appliqué. See drawing below.

base fabric

Lightweight background fabric, interfacing on the reverse side, securely tacked to the base

..now a firm base for the appliqué...

...ready to stitch....

APPLIQUÉ FABRICS

Dressweight cottons are best for appliqué shapes, ideal are American 100 per cent cotton prints and plains (solids) often used for patchwork and widely available. These cottons come in a dazzling array of designs and colours and are easy to use.

When selecting fabrics be aware of how printed designs can work for you. For example, a green leafy print may be idea as tree foliage, a geometric design for a garden path or wall. Sometimes a particular print or colour may be irresistible and you could decide to base a whole design around the fabric. If a lightweight cotton catches your eye as being the perfect background, use the suggested method given above to prepare it for appliqué. For guidance on backing fabrics refer to pages 25–6.

Very little of the fabric you buy need be wasted.

WARNING : IT IS EASY TO BECOME A FABRICHOLIC . BUT SUCH A JOY !

It is easy to justify purchasing beautiful, colourful, fabulous fabrics if you think of all the future projects you will use them for.

Use the initial design as a guide to what fabrics are needed. Work out how many different fabrics are required and the quantities. Each project featured in the book gives guidelines to the amount of fabric needed. Leftovers from each one go into the collection!

Remember, when storing fabrics, that humidity and direct sunlight are their worst enemies and will have a destructive effect over the years.

'BUT I CAN'T DRAW!'

Many people feel they cannot draw, but for the beginner the need to draw is not important. As you begin to sketch or trace your designs, you should gradually gain confidence with pencil and paper, overcoming any hesitancy. You will probably be surprised at a newfound ability – draw and enjoy it! Anxiety will disappear.

Initially, using the suggested sources (page 11), look for a picture on which you would like to base your design, remembering the emphasis on simplicity. This picture can be copied freehand, traced or photocopied. If you want the picture to be larger, many photocopiers can do this easily. Enlarging by hand and eye yourself can give slightly imperfect shapes in your picture, although this irregularity has lots of charm and can enhance your work.

There are ways around any lack of expertise with a pencil, but practising from the start will give confidence and, hopefully, enable you to draw your own designs at a later stage.

For each project you will need two full-sized copies of the design, that is to the actual size of the finished piece of work. One will act as a reference guide, the other will be cut up to use as templates. As you gain experience you can abandon templates, drawing the shapes freehand on the wrong side of the fabrics.

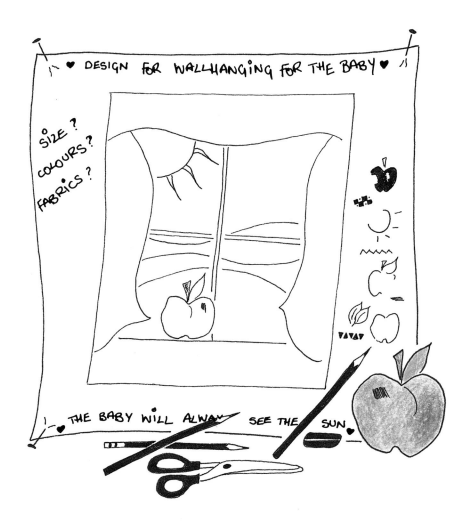

PRE-STITCHING PREPARATION

·COLOURS ARE REAL IN DAYLIGHT.

Draw two full-sized images of your design using one of the methods suggested on page 16.

Wash your selected fabrics, including those to be used for the base and/or background. This prevents any shrinkage and/or dye runs occurring when the finished item is washed. Avoid biological washing powders and liquids. Wash dressweight cottons by hand in hot water, then rinse them in equally hot water to remove any loose dye – this will also show you which fabrics have loose dyes. Rinse fabrics with loose dye until the rinse water becomes clear, then hang them to dry on the washing line. Iron your fabrics ready for use and keep clean and fresh in plastic bags.

Apply vilene (pellon) to the wrong side of the chosen appliqué fabrics, following the manufacturer's instructions. Only cut and back the amount of fabric needed for your project, and set aside any left over.

Select the threads you need.

Base/background fabric. Cut a piece larger than you need and tack the perimeter area of your design onto it. This defines the area to be appliquéd, and will help you keep to the planned dimensions. As you gain confidence you may want your boundaries to be flexible and your work to develop a size of its own as you progress. In this case just start with a larger piece of fabric.

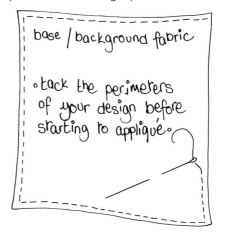

base / background fabric

∘ tack the perimeters of your design before starting to appliqué.

With garments, the appliqué is stitched onto the appropriate section of the garment, before it is made up.

Make sure your working surfaces are clean – now it is time to begin cutting out your shapes!

CUTTING OUT THE FABRIC SHAPES

If the fabrics to be used for the appliqué shapes have vilene (pellon) on their reverse sides, the shapes can be cut out. Cut your templates from one of the full-sized drawings you have prepared, noting the places where the shapes overlap or underlap each other, and perhaps marking those places on the reference drawing and the templates. You could also mark the stitching order on the drawing or templates. These preparations are useful when cutting out and stitching. To use the project templates on pages 94–117, refer to the notes on page 92.

Vilene (pellon) is ironed onto the reverse side of a fabric to stabilize it, so that you can cut out the shapes with the grain of the fabric going in any direction. At this stage be aware that sometimes the templates may have to be placed upside-down on the interfaced side of the fabric, enabling the shape to be the correct way round for stitching.

Draw around your template on the reverse (interfaced) side of the fabric using a soft pencil. Cut out the shape. Alternatively, pin the template to the right side of the fabric and cut around it.

shape reversed onto wrong side of fabric. extra fabric to be cut to allow for underlap

the drawing : underlaps indicated on each section with arrows. sections numbered in stitching order

the drawing is cut up to make the templates

If you want to draw the shapes freehand, use a soft pencil and draw on the interfaced side of the fabric. Cut out.

Check you have allowed extra fabric for underlaps. Should you make a mistake, the fabric shapes can be juggled about to accommodate this before stitching. Sometimes this can be a real advantage as you may gain a slightly different and more interesting effect than the one planned. If you have several templates from one drawing, number the templates and the corresponding shapes on your reference drawing, then number the fabric shapes as you cut each one out. This eliminates any confusion when all the shapes have been cut out. Fabric snippets stuck onto the relevant places on your reference drawing, make another useful guide.

Do not forget that shapes, colours and fabrics can be altered, modified or moved until you feel pleased and satisfied with the arrangement. You will discover that the creative process is a true pleasure.

After your shapes have been cut out, collect the fabric off-cuts and save them for future projects. You never know when that tiny piece of fabric, which looks too small to be useful, may be just what you need.

STITCHING TECHNIQUES

.the stitch covers the raw edge.

.alter the stitch width and length to suit your requirements and preference.

As previously explained, satin stitch is used to apply all the shapes. The stitch width most frequently used is 4, but this is reduced for smaller shapes, when a wide stitch is obviously going to be too large. The stitch length is usually between ½ and 1, depending on your machine, your requirement and your preference.

If the lower thread on your machine does not pull through to the corners of the upper stitches, you can use the same colour thread in the bobbin for all your stitching. Change only the top thread to match the colours of your fabrics. If the lower thread does pull through to the top, even a little, use the same colour on the bobbin that you use on the top.

The most frequently used size of needle is no 80 (11), but for fine fabrics or tiny shapes no 70 (9) is worth trying.

You are now ready to begin applying the appliqué shapes. Read through this section explaining the techniques, then practise them before you start stitching your first project. Tack (baste) your first shape in place onto the base/

background fabric. Do not pin it as the shape will move. Start stitching with the appliqué shape to the right or left of the machine foot. Stitch with the foot of the sewing machine down on the fabric. The needle goes into the fabric at the edge of the shape and stitches over onto it, covering the raw edge. The stitches look neatest if they are at right angles to the edge of the appliqué shape, not slanting along it.

.stitching with the shape to your left.

A long gradual curve requires the fabric to be gently eased round with your fingers on the work, enabling you to stitch the curve evenly.

If you reach a place that is too rounded to stitch in one flowing movement, stop with the needle *in* the fabric. The needle can be either on the inner or outer edge of the stitch line depending on the direction of the curve. Lift the foot and pivot the work slightly to alter the line of stitching to accommodate the curve, put the foot down and continue. You may need to do this several times around one curve. Pivoting enables the stitching to remain even around awkward curves, and the raw edges to be covered.

.stitching with the shape to your right.

·ease the fabric around the curve·

·leave the needle in the fabric·

·lift the foot·
·pivot the fabric on the needle·

·needle down· foot up·

·pivot the fabric on the needle·
·foot down ·stitch up the next side·

round ninety degrees ready to stitch up the next side, lower the foot and continue.

Points are approached in the same way as corners, and this method gives a very acceptable finish. Alternatively, the width of the stitch may be reduced gradually down to 1 or ½ as you approach the point, pivot with the needle in the point, then increase the stitch width gradually up to the original setting as you stitch up the other side of the shape. If your machine does not allow this gradual smooth change of stitch width, use the first method. When you have finished stitching, leave the ends of the threads long, pull them through to the reverse side of the work, knot at the beginning and end of the stitch line. If the line of stitches ends where it began, take a few extra stitches over those already there, pull the threads through to the back and finish off.

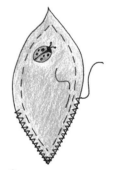

·point stitched in the same way as a corner.

·stitched with stitch width reducing to the point then increasing again.

The same pivoting technique applies on corners. When your stitching reaches a corner, leave the needle in the work, lift the foot, turn the fabric

You may feel that some areas of your work need pressing when they have been completed. Do this very cautiously, perhaps covering the area with a tea towel and ironing on top of this. Sometimes pressing the back of the work is best. Whichever way you press the work, beware of pressing an area of fabric which has the stitch line of another shape running underneath it. This can make an unsightly shiny mark on the top of your work.

It is not necessary to satin stitch the raw edge of a shape which is to be covered by another shape overlapping it. Leave the tacking (basting) in place until the shape is secured, and then remove.

If your project is large, and therefore unwieldy when being guided through the gap between the needle and the body of the machine, the fabric can be rolled up, leaving flat only the section to be stitched. The fabric is unrolled and rearranged as stitching progresses. In this way, a larger piece of work becomes manageable.

If the fabric is too bulky for this method, the project will have to be made in separate blocks and stitched together when the appliqué is completed (Partly Patchwork Cushion page 86 uses this technique). As you progress with your work, it is often extremely valuable to pin the piece up, step back and look at it from a distance. Then leave it for a while and come back again with eyes refreshed.

FINISHING

WALLHANGINGS

Wallhangings can be finished with a contrasting fabric border stitched around the four edges of the design. Lightweight cottons are suitable for this, although some cottons are more opaque and firmer if vilene (pellon) is applied to them. Decide whether or not you want to use vilene (pellon) before cutting out the border.

Cut four strips of fabric the desired border width, plus a 6mm (¼in) seam allowance, and longer than the outside edge measurements of the finished piece of work. With right sides together, tack (baste) a strip along one vertical edge of the work, and another along the opposite edge. Straight stitch along the seamline, fold the strips back and press. Cut off the excess fabric.

the two remaining border strips are tacked (basted) in place, stitched & pressed back

opposite border strips are tacked (basted) in place, stitched, then pressed back

Tack (baste) the two remaining strips along the two horizontal edges of the wallhanging, covering the top and bottom raw edges of the border strips already in place. Straight stitch and press back. The borders are now complete.

Most of the wallhanging projects in this book are hung from loops stitched into the top of the hanging or from a casing sewn along the back. A rod is threaded through the loops or casing, and a

cord attached to the rod.

For each loop, cut a length of about 14cm (5½in) and double the preferred width, plus 6mm (¼in) seam allowances. With right sides together, straight stitch lengthways down the strip, leaving the ends open, to form a tube.

the strip of fabric for the loops is folded in half & stitched down its length to form a tube

Pull through to the right side and press, with the seam down the centre. Topstitching 6mm (¼in) in from each edge gives a professional finish, but is not essential.

Pull the fabric through to the right side, press with the seam along the centre back. top stitch if preferred

Repeat this process making several loops all the same size, (the actual number will vary depending on the size of the wallhanging and your preference). Fold the loops in half, raw edges together with the seams inside, and space them evenly along the top front edge of the wallhanging, raw edges upwards. Tack (baste) firmly in place.

the loops are spaced evenly along the top of the work & tacked (basted) in place

When the backing fabric is stitched in place, the loops are attached securely into the same seam and will appear in the correct position when the work is turned through to the right side.

the work is turned through to the right side & the loops appear in their correct places

A casing is added after the backing is in place. Cut a strip from the backing fabric approximately 6.5cm (2½in) wide and the same length as the width of the wallhanging. Along both sides of the length of the strip, fold under 6mm (¼in) of

the fabric and press. Now pin the casing onto the backing, about 4cm (1½in) down from the top edge. Turn the sides of the casing under so that it is about 4mm (1½in) in from both edges of the wallhanging.

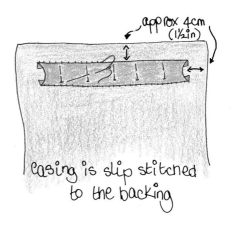

approx 4cm (1½in)

casing is slip stitched to the backing

Attach the casing loosely to the backing using slip stitch along the top and bottom edges. It should not be completely flat against the backing, to allow the rod to sit without distorting the fabric of the wallhanging.

Lightweight cottons or calico (muslin) are ideal for the backing. Cut the fabric to the same size as the finished piece of work and, with right sides together, lay it over the work. Pin, then tack (baste) together. Straight stitch around the outside edge with a 6–12mm (¼–½in) seam, leaving an opening at the base.

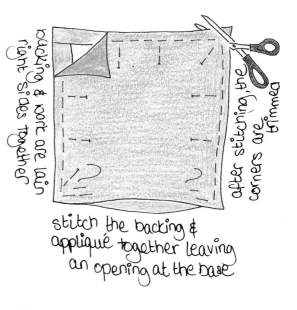

backing & work are laid right sides together

after stitching, the corners are trimmed

stitch the backing & appliqué together leaving an opening at the base

Trim the corners, then carefully ease the whole

wallhanging through the opening. The right sides will now be on the outside. Close the opening by slip stitching the edges. The wallhanging is now ready to display. Make a rod from wooden dowelling available from most hardware shops. It can be left natural, stained or painted as you prefer.

CUSHIONS

Complete the appliqué on the cushion front. The loose ends on the reverse side of the work can be hidden by covering with a piece of lightweight calico (muslin) or similar fabric. This is subsequently stitched into the seam to secure it. Select which fabric you want to use for the cushion back. This could be the same fabric as the background of the appliqué, although lightweight cottons, calico (muslin) and furnishing fabrics are all suitable.

It is not necessary to pipe cushions, but it does give a professional finish to your work and is a useful technique to learn. A length of fabric-covered piping cord is stitched into the seam when the front and back of the cushion are joined, and appears in the seamline when the work is turned through (see Alphabetical Cushions page 33). The colour chosen for the piping can contrast or tone with the cushion, to outline or enhance the appliqué. Use medium to lightweight fabric, the cushion backing fabric or even the appliqué cottons.

Buy enough piping cord of the preferred size to fit around the perimeter of the cushion, with some to spare. You need a strip of fabric the same length as the cord, either in one piece or made from several lengths joined together, which is more economical. If possible, cut the fabric strip on the cross grain, but this is not essential. The strip needs to be about 4cm (1½in) wide or more, depending on which size cord you use. If joining lengths of fabric together to make the strip, cut them all with the grain the same way, and stitch them together with a seam going diagonally across the strip. This makes the seamline more flexible and less visible. A patchwork effect can be created by using different coloured fabrics, stitched together to make the long strip. This is an appealing way of outlining your appliqué.

Fold the fabric, wrong sides together, around the cord to encase it. Tack (baste) the two raw edges together, as close to the cord as you can, to hold it in place within the fold.

piping cord is laid along the wrong side of the strip. fabric folded over it. raw edges come together. tack close to the cord

Tack (baste) the prepared piping around the edge of the cushion front on the seamline, raw edges facing outwards and the piping inwards. To ease the piping around the corners, clip the fabric, not the cord.

the strips of fabric are joined, right sides together, with a diagonal seamline. trim the fabric press the seam

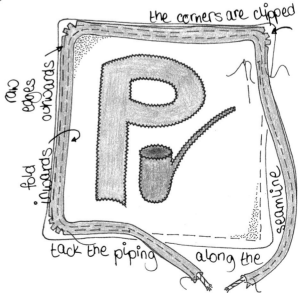

the corners are clipped

raw edges outwards

fold inwards

tack the piping along the seamline

The cushion front is now ready for its backing. All the cushion projects in this book use the envelope method. You will need some fabric large enough to cut into two pieces, which overlap one another by about 15cm (6in) and includes a 12mm (½in) seam allowance all around the outside edge (see drawing below). When complete the envelope back should be the same size as the cushion front.

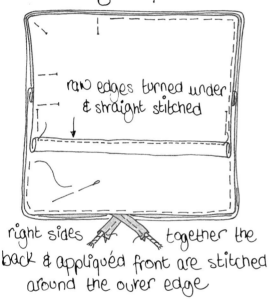

two pieces of fabric overlap by about 15cm (6in) & together form the cushion back

raw edges turned under & straight stitched

right sides together the back & appliquéd front are stitched around the outer edge

Turn under and straight stitch the overlap edges to neaten and prevent them fraying. With right sides together, pin the two pieces of fabric onto the front of the cushion, ensuring that the neatened edges overlap. Tack (baste) the cushion front and back together, checking that the raw edges of the piping are taken into the seam. Use the zip foot on your sewing machine and straight stitch through all the layers, as close to the piping cord as possible but not over it, easing the stitching around the corners.

Trim away any excess fabric and neaten the raw edges of the cushion cover. Turn the cover through to the right side. Remove the tacking (basting) thread, and slide the cushion pad in through the opening.

If the cushion is to be a gift, a special message could be written using a waterproof ink pen, on a piece of prepared appliqué fabric, and slip stitched to the backing.

BAGS

Complete the appliqué on the two bag panels. To give the bag a soft, padded appearance and feel, insert wadding (batting) between the bag panels and the lining, and inside the handles. If you are using wadding (batting), cut two pieces the same size as the bag panels, place each piece behind a panel. This is an additional layer to be taken in when you stitch the seam around the edge of the bag. With right sides of the bag panels together, stitch the two sides and the base. Turn through so that the right sides come to the outside, wadding (batting), if used, inside.

Decide on the width and length of the handles and cut two pieces of fabric the appropriate size. Using the same method as for the wallhanging loops (page 24), make two handles. Insert wadding (batting), if used, into the centre of the handles before topstitching. Making sure that the outside edges of both handles are the same distance from the outside edges of the bag, pin and tack (baste) the handles in place on the right sides of the panels, upside-down, raw edges upwards and the centre seams facing outwards.

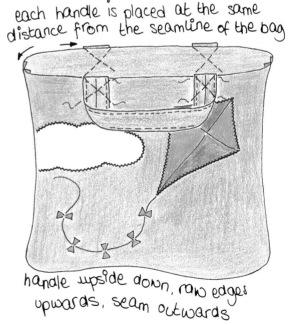

each handle is placed at the same distance from the seamline of the bag

handle upside down, raw edges upwards, seam outwards

Make another 'bag' the same size as the one to be lined from the selected lining fabric, check that the circumference around the top is the same. Keep the lining inside out after stitching the seams, and slide over the bag so that the lining and bag are right sides together, and the appliqué and handles are covered. Pin and tack (baste) the top raw edges together.

slide the lining over the bag, right sides together, covering the appliqué & handles

Straight stitch around the top, 12mm (½in) below the raw edges, securing the handles in the

seam. Leave an opening of about 15cm (6in) in the stitch line.

stitch around the top leaving a gap in the seam

Insert your hand into the opening and ease the bag out through the gap, bringing the right side to the outside. Push the lining down into the centre of the bag. Remove the tacking (basting) from the handles, which will now stand upright. Slip stitch the opening closed.

remove the tacking (basting) from the handles. slip stitch the opening closed

HAPPY HEARTS
WALLHANGINGS

These small wallhangings are ideal as a gift for a special person, perhaps sent as an unusual Valentine card? They can be made in whatever colours you fancy, chosen from the fabulous range of plain (solid) fabrics available. The colours shown here make soft pastel hearts, but they could be made in truly vibrant hues. Very easy to make, the four wallhangings look striking displayed together – an original way to express and send a message of love.

APPROXIMATE FINISHED SIZE: 18 × 19cm (7 × 7½in)

For four wallhangings you will need:
♥   25cm (¼yd) medium-weight base/background fabric, 115cm (45in) wide, eg calico (muslin)
♥   Six 25cm (¼yd) lengths appliqué fabric, 115cm (45in) wide, in assorted plain (solid) colours, for the backing, hearts and borders.
♥   Threads to match the appliqué fabrics
♥   25cm (¼yd) thin polyester wadding (batting)
♥   Eight small brass rings and cord for hanging

1   Prepare your fabrics as described in Pre-stitching Preparation (page 17).

2   Cut four pieces of base/background fabric 19×20cm (7½×8in), this includes a seam allowance of 6mm (¼in).

· background/base fabric cut to finished size + 6mm (¼in) seam allowance · the hearts are tacked (basted) in position.

3   Cut eight heart shapes from your chosen appliqué fabrics using the templates on page 93. The shapes may be regular or irregular as you prefer.

4   Tack (baste) the shapes in position on your base/background fabric (see drawing above).

5   Satin stitch around the shapes, the larger hearts first. Stitch round the smaller hearts using a slightly reduced stitch width.

satin stitch around the larger heart first

6   Remove the tacking (basting) and very gently press the back of the each wallhanging.

7   Make four border strips each 4cm (1½in) wide × 21cm (8in) long for each wallhanging. Do this by cutting the coloured appliqué fabrics into short unequal lengths all 4cm (1½in) wide. Sew several of these lengths together with 6mm (¼in) seams to make each 21cm (8in) long multi-

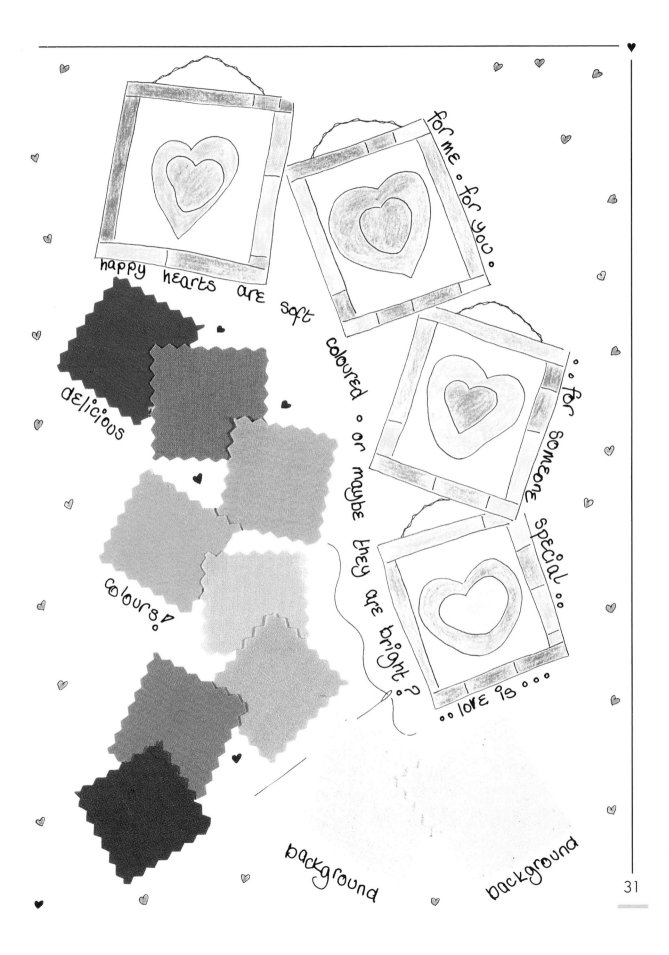

happy hearts are soft

for me · for you ·

coloured · or maybe they are bright?

delicious

colours?

· · for someone special · ·

· · love is · · ·

background

background

coloured strip. Press open the seams.

random lengths of fabric joined to make, a colourful border for the appliqué

8 With right sides together, tack the two side strips into position so that the edge of the border is 2.5cm (1in) in from the raw edge of the wallhanging (see drawing below). Repeat for the other three wallhangings. Complete the borders as described in Finishing (page 24).

the border is machine stitched in place, folded back so that the raw edges come together, and pressed. the top and bottom strips are then sewn in place.

9 Cut four pieces of wadding (batting) slightly larger than each wallhanging. Lay each wallhanging on top of a piece of wadding (batting).

10 Choose the colour fabrics you wish to use for your backing. Follow the procedure described in Finishing (page 24), cut out and complete the backing for each wallhanging, stitching in the wadding (batting) at the same time.

11 Stitch two brass rings onto the back of each wallhanging, tie on the cord.

·the appliqué is laid on top of the wadding·

·machine stitch through the the three layers, leaving an opening· trim the corners·

♥ for a special person ♥

·brass rings are sewn on the back· the cord attached·

ALPHABETICAL
CUSHIONS

These cushions add fun, colour and life to a room. Made to spell a child's name or with the recipient's initial appliquéd on the front, they are an ideal gift and a very simple project for beginners. Many different shapes can be used alongside the letters – perhaps the simple outline of a child's best-loved toy or an adult's favourite flower?

FINISHED SIZE: 30 × 30cm (12 × 12in)

For three 30cm (12in) square cushions you will need:

🤍   1m (1yd) firm cotton fabric, 115cm (45in) wide, for the base/background (forms cushion fronts and backs)

🤍   25cm (¼yd) appliqué fabric, 115cm (45in) wide, for the letters and piping

🤍   Four 25cm (¼yd) lengths appliqué fabric, 115cm (45in) wide, in plain (solid) colours, for the motifs and piping

🤍   4.5m (5yd) thin piping cord
🤍   Threads to match the appliqué fabrics
🤍   Three 30cm (12in) square cushion pads

1   Prepare your fabrics as described in Pre-stitching Preparation (page 17).

2   Cut out three 36cm (14in) squares from the base/background fabric. Tack (baste) the outline of a 30cm (12in) square onto each piece and appliqué within them.

3   Cut out all the appliqué shapes using the templates on pages 94–6.

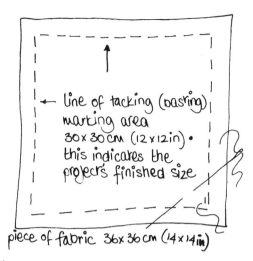

4 Tack (baste) the letters in place on the squares of base/background fabric. Satin stitch around them, except for the areas overlapped by the shapes. Refer to Stitching Techniques (page 22).

• the letters are tacked (basted) onto the background/base fabric then satin stitched in place.

5 **Cushion A** Tack (baste) the apple and leaves into position. Satin stitch around them. A short line of close satin stitches creates the stalk.

Cushion B Tack (baste) the two lower segments of the wings into position. Satin stitch around all but the top edges as these will be covered and secured by the upper wing segments (see drawing below). Tack (baste) the upper segments into position. Satin stitch around them.

Apply the body. The antennae are straight machine stitches.

Cushion C Tack (baste) the cat into place. Satin stitch around it. The whiskers are straight machine stitches.

no need to satin stitch these edges

each section of the butterfly numbered according to order of stitching • n° 1 is first to be stitched

6 Neaten the thread ends as described in Stitching Techniques (page 22) and press the cushions if required.

7 Cover piping cord and attach to the cushions as described in Finishing (page 26).

8 To complete your cushions, cut out and sew on the backs as described in Finishing (page 27).

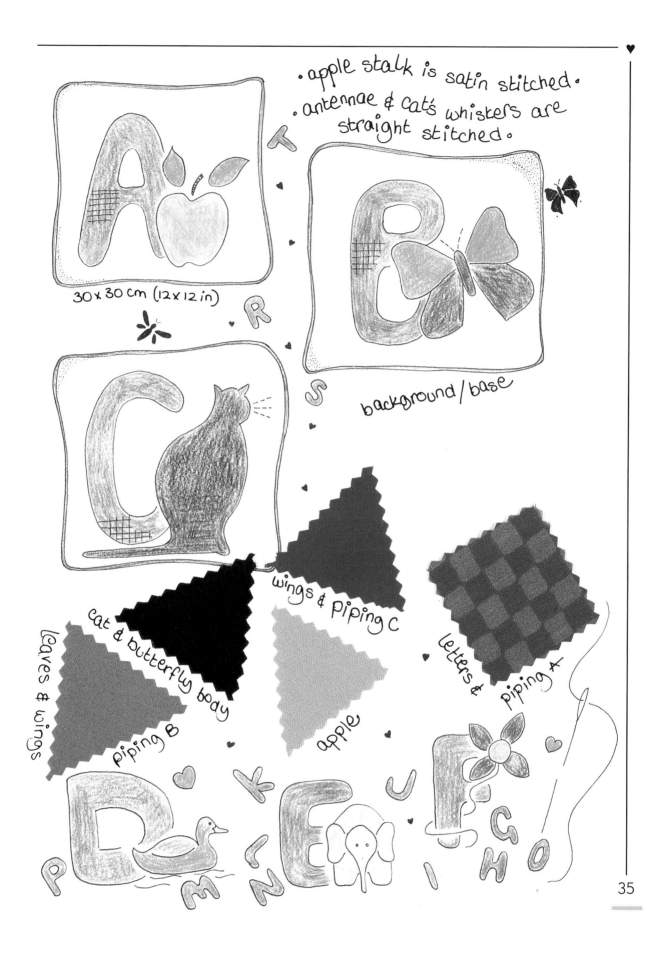

- apple stalk is satin stitched.
- antennae & cat's whiskers are straight stitched.

30 × 30 cm (12 × 12 in)

background/base

wings & piping C

cat & butterfly body

leaves & wings

piping B

apple

letters & piping A

35

WALLHANGINGS BY
NUMBERS

*These stimulating wallhangings are both educational and decorative –
ideal for a nursery or playroom, with their bright colours and simple shapes.
They could be adapted to mark a birthday or anniversary, with colourful
shapes appropriate to the occasion. Very easy to make, the wallhangings
are hung from dowelling rods and painted with acrylic paints.*

FINISHED SIZE: *33 × 33cm (13 × 13in)*

For three wallhangings you will need:
♥ 1m (1yd) lightweight calico (muslin), 115cm (45in) wide, for the base and backing
♥ Three 50cm (½yd) lengths appliqué fabric, 115cm (45in) wide, in different colours, for the backgrounds, borders and loops
♥ 25cm (¼yd) appliqué fabric, 115cm (45in) wide, for the numbers
♥ Small pieces of appliqué fabrics in assorted colours, for the shapes and loops
♥ Threads to match the appliqué fabrics
♥ Rods and cords for hanging

1 Prepare your fabrics as described in Pre-stitching Preparation (page 17).

2 Cut three 32cm (12½in) squares from the calico (muslin). Cut three squares the same size from the background fabrics and tack (baste) onto the base calico (muslin). See Fabrics (page 14).

3 Cut the numbers and shapes from the chosen appliqué fabrics using the templates on pages 97–8. Tack (baste) the numbers in position on the background fabrics. Satin stitch in place, except for the areas to be overlapped. Refer to Stitching Techniques (page 22).

4 **Wallhanging No. 1.** Tack (baste) the tree trunk. Satin stitch in place, except for the areas to be overlapped. Apply the tree top, covering the top of the trunk.
  Wallhanging No. 2. Tack (baste) then satin stitch, the clouds into position.
  Wallhanging No. 3. Tack (baste), then satin stitch the flowers, then apply the centres.

the trunk is appliquéd in position
the tree top is then tacked (basted)
to the background to cover the
top of the tree trunk

5 Cut the border strips. For each wallhanging you will need four strips in the selected border colour, 36cm (14in) long × 4cm (1½in) wide. This width allows for a 6mm (¼in) seam giving a finished border width of about 2.5cm (1in). Stitch on the borders to the completed appliquéd squares as described in Finishing (page 24).

6 Make the loops and tack (baste) in place as described in Finishing (page 24).

7 Follow the procedure described in Finishing (page 24), to cut out and complete the backing for each wallhanging.

8 Thread the rods through the loops and attach the cord.

33 x 33 cm (12x12 in)

clouds

numbers

background & border

tree

background & border

flowers

background & border

♥ rods painted with acrylic paint

♥ white cord for hanging

♥ happy colours!

SUMMER VIEW
WALLHANGING

Do you have a favourite scene, a remembered image, or a photograph of a view, which you would enjoy translating into fabrics? They can be simplified into a design as clear as this one to create a charming, evocative wallhanging. Although simple to make, this project introduces appliquéing a narrow strip of fabric and small rounded shapes.

FINISHED SIZE: 32 × 37cm (12½ × 14½in)

♥ 50cm (½yd) lightweight calico (muslin), 115cm (45in) wide, for the base, backing and casing

♥ 50cm (19in) square blue appliqué fabric, for the sky

♥ Four 20cm (8in) lengths appliqué fabric, 115cm (45in) wide, for the hills and fields

♥ 20cm (8in) white appliqué fabric, 115cm (45in) wide, for the windowsill and frame

♥ 25cm (¼yd) appliqué fabric, 115cm (45in) wide, for the curtains

♥ Two small pieces appliqué fabric in different colours, for the vase and flowers

♥ Threads to match the appliqué fabrics

♥ Rod and cords for hanging.

1 Prepare your fabrics as described in Pre-Stitching Preparation (page 17).

2 Cut a piece of calico 33×38cm (13×15in). Tack (baste) the blue sky fabric over the calico (muslin) base, creating the blue background for the appliqué. Refer to Fabrics (page 14).

3 Cut out all the appliqué shapes using the templates on page 99. You will also to need to cut out from the white appliqué fabric: one strip 6mm (¼in) wide, about 17cm (6¾in) long, for the vertical window frame; one strip 12mm (½in) wide for the horizontal window frame; one strip 6cm (2½in) wide for the windowsill.
Draw the hills and fields freehand, on the back of the fabrics and cut out.

4 Tack (baste), then satin stitch the shapes into position one by one, remembering to leave the

areas to be overlapped. Refer to Stitching Techniques (page 22). Apply the cloud, the hills, then the fields.

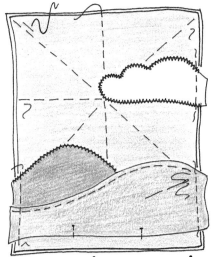

in the appropriate order, stitch the hills onto the background and the scene evolves

Next apply the window frames and windowsill, the two curtains, followed by the pelmet. Then the vase and lastly the flowers.

5 Follow the procedure described in Finishing (page 24) to cut out and complete the backing and casing.

6 Thread the rod through the casing and attach the cord.

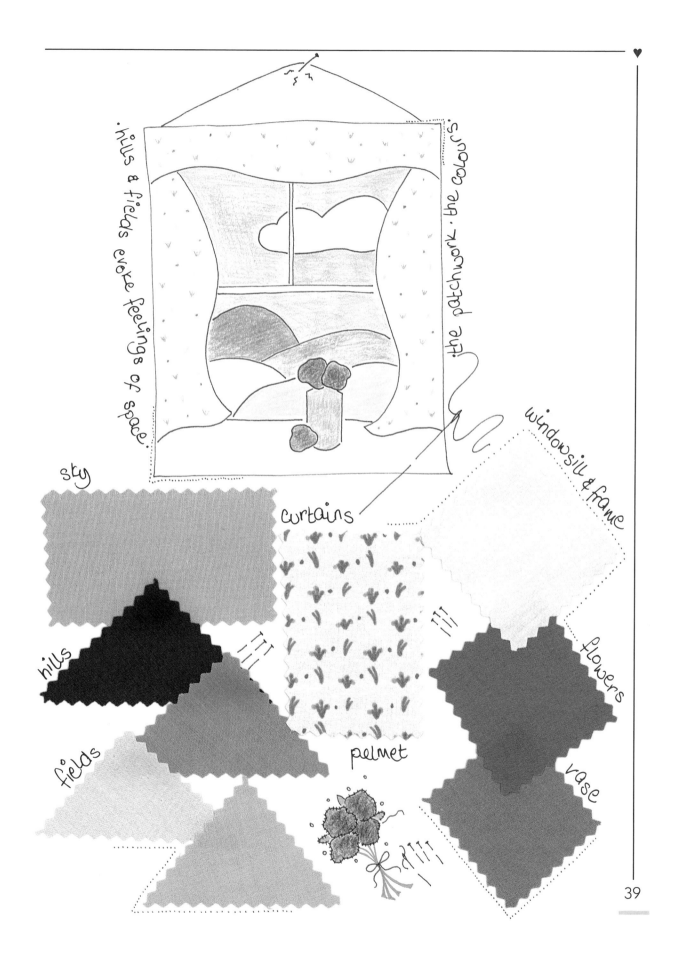

· hills & fields evoke feelings of space ·

· the patchwork · the colours ·

sky

curtains

windowsill & frame

hills

flowers

fields

pelmet

vase

39

SPACIOUS SHOEBAG

This capacious shoebag will look bright and amusing wherever it hangs. Easy to make in ticking (pillow ticking), it is durable and washes well. Use it for shoes, sports kit, as a child's overnight bag or, if you are a traveller, to pack your shoes and protect your clothes from dusty footwear. An initial could be appliquéd alongside the boots to personalize the bag. All the detailing on the boots is machine stitched, a practice useful for future projects.

FINISHED SIZE: *37 × 41cm (14¹/₂ × 16in)*

♥ 50cm (½yd) ticking (pillow ticking), 150cm (60in) wide

♥ Two 25cm (¼yd) lengths appliqué fabric, 115cm (45in) wide, for the boots

♥ 10cm (4in) white appliqué fabric, 115cm (45in) wide, for the boot trims

♥ Threads to match the appliqué fabrics

♥ 1.5cm (1½yd) cord

♥ Large eyelets (available as a kit)

1 Prepare your fabrics as described in Pre-Stitching Preparation (page 17).

2 Cut a piece of ticking (pillow ticking) 82×86cm (32¼×34in). Position the appliqué so that when the bag is complete, the design is on one side only.

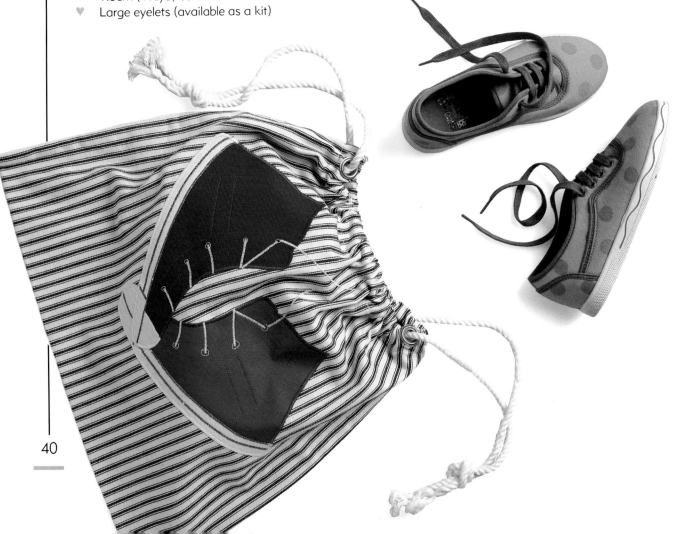

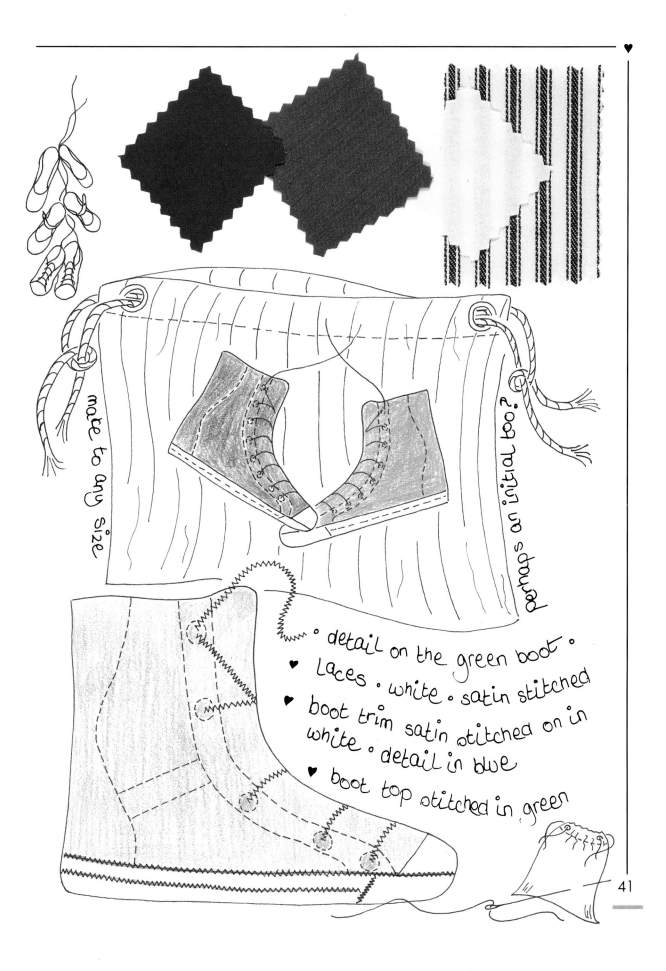

mate to any size

perhaps an initial too?

○ detail on the green boot ○
♥ laces ○ white ○ satin stitched
♥ boot trim satin stitched on in white ○ detail in blue
♥ boot top stitched in green

41

3   Cut out all the appliqué shapes using the templates on page 100. The boot details (see worksheet right) may be machine stitched onto the shapes before or after they are appliquéd to the ticking (pillow ticking). Tack (baste) the green boot in place first, satin stitch the top and sides, then add the white trim to overlap the base of the boot. Satin stitch in place, except for the areas to be overlapped. Refer to Stitching Techniques (page 22). The green boot has blue topstitched detail on the white trim. Apply the blue boot in the same way, and add green topstitching to the white trim (see worksheet page 41).

4   With the appliqué complete, make the shoebag using French seams. With right sides outwards, fold the ticking (pillow ticking) in half, and machine stitch a 6mm (¼in) seam down each side. Trim. Turn inside out so that the right sides come together. Make a second 6mm (¼in) seam down each side, which encloses the first, machine stitching the two sides together (see drawings below).

5   Following the eyelet kit instructions, insert the four eyelets into the ticking (pillow ticking), one on each side of the seams, about 4cm (1½in) down from the raw edge and about 2.5cm (1in) either side of the seams.

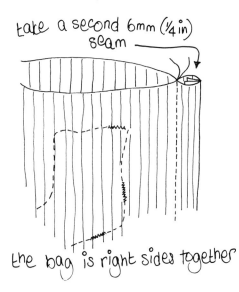

take a second 6mm (¼in) seam

the bag is right sides together

6   Fold the top 5cm (2in) of the bag inwards, to below the eyelets. Turn under a 6–12mm (¼–½in) seam along the raw edge. Stitch along the folded edge under the eyelets, making a 3cm (1½in) casing for the cord. Cut the cord in half, thread one half into the casing through one of the eyelets, pull the cord round and out again at the adjacent eyelet, and knot the two loose ends. Repeat this procedure with the other piece of cord, threading through the opposite two eyelets.

the cord is threaded through the casing ∘ the ends are knotted

make a 6mm (¼in) seam down each side of the bag ∘ right sides outside

(*right*) Flying Kites Wallhanging and Sun, Sea and Sand Bag

SUMMER TWILIGHT
WALLHANGING

Create this colourful wallhanging which is striking in its simplicity. It is basically the same design as the Summer View Wallhanging (page 38), and illustrates how a very different result can be achieved by altering colours, the hills and the motifs. Wadding (batting) is used behind the lightweight cotton base fabric, so that when the appliqué shapes are applied a slightly puffy effect is created. This quilted look gives a soft dimension to the completed work, which is easy to make.

FINISHED SIZE: 46 × 40cm (18 × 15½in)

♥ 50cm (½yd) appliqué fabric, 115cm (45in) wide, for the base/background, backing and casing

♥ 50cm (½yd) lightweight polyester wadding (batting), 115cm (45in) wide

♥ 25cm (¼yd) appliqué fabric, 115cm (45in) wide, for the curtains

♥ Four 6.5 x 40cm (2½ × 15½in) scraps appliqué fabric, for the hills and apple leaves

♥ 11 × 6.5cm (4½ × 2½in) piece appliqué fabric, for the sun

♥ 25cm (¼yd) appliqué fabric, 115cm (45in) wide, for the windowsill, frames and moon

♥ 10cm (4in) appliqué fabric, 115cm (45in) wide, for the apples.

♥ Threads to match the appliqué fabrics. Brown thread for the apple stalks

♥ Rod and cord for hanging

1 Prepare your fabrics as described in Pre-Stitching Preparation (page 17).

2 Cut out the base/background fabric and wadding (batting) to the required size. Tack (baste) the base/background fabric to the wadding (batting), creating a firm base for the appliqué.

3 Cut out all the appliqué shapes using the templates on pages 99 and 100. Use the curtains, pelmet and windowsill from the Summer View

Wallhanging, enlarging them a little. For the window frame cut four strips all 1cm (⅜in) wide, two 40cm (15½in) long, two 22cm (8½in) long. Draw the hills freehand, on the back of the fabrics, cut out the shapes. The sun is a semi-circle. For the whole apple use the template from the Bag of Fruit (page 104).

4 Tack (baste), then satin stitch the shapes remembering to leave the areas to be overlapped. Refer to Stitching Techniques (page 22). First the sun and moon, then the hills overlapping each other, the hill nearest the sun first. The windowsill completes this sequence.

5 Satin stitch the sun's rays in the thread used for the appliqué (see worksheet right).

6 Apply the window frame, the apples and their leaves. The apple stalks are satin stitched using brown thread.

7 Finally apply the curtains and pelmet to finish the appliqué.

8 Follow the procedure described in Finishing (page 24) to cut out and complete the backing and casing.

9 Thread the rod through the casing and attach the cord.

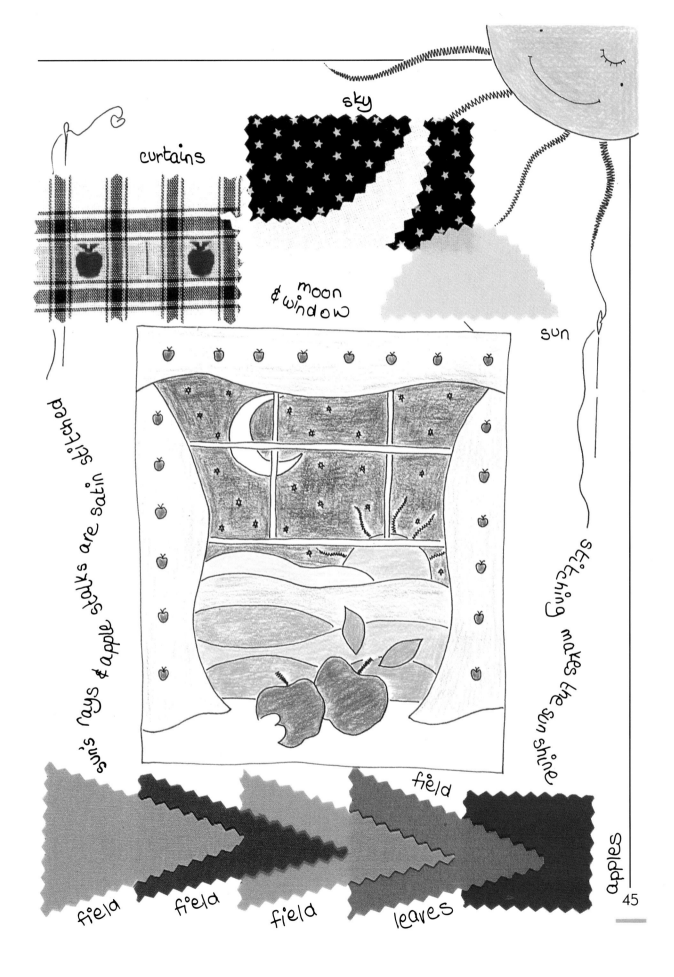

curtains

sky

moon
& window

sun

sun's rays & apple stalks are satin stitched

stitching makes the sun shine

field

field

field

field

leaves

apples

45

TABITHA TEDDY
CUSHION

Slip a message, coin or even a tooth for the tooth fairy into the pocket on Tabitha's dress. This easy-to-make cushion can be complemented by a co-ordinating cot quilt (page 56), whilst the shoe bag (page 40) enlarged and appliquéd with teddy instead of the shoes, becomes a matching laundry or toy bag. Teddy may wear a frock or dungarees and the appliqué looks particularly effective when primary colours are combined with the softer brown tones of the teddy. The face is hand embroidered with black embroidery thread to add the finishing touches.

FINISHED SIZE: *30 × 30cm (12 × 12in)*

♥ 50cm (½yd) medium-weight calico (muslin), 137cm (54in) wide, for the base/background (forms the cushion front and back)
♥ 10cm (4in) appliqué fabric, 115cm (45in) wide, for the teddy
♥ Two 15cm (6in) squares appliqué fabric, for teddy's dress and pocket
♥ 25cm (¼yd) lightweight cotton fabric, 115cm (45in) wide, for the piping
♥ Threads to match the appliqué fabrics
♥ Black embroidery thread
♥ 1.5m (1½yd) piping cord
♥ 30cm (12in) square cushion pad

1 Prepare your fabrics as described in Pre-stitching Preparation (page 17).

2 Cut out a 36cm (14in) square from the base/background fabric. Tack (baste) the outline of a 30cm (12in) square onto the fabric, appliqué within it.

3 Cut out all the appliqué shapes using the templates on page 101.

4 Tack (baste) and satin stitch the arms and legs in place, except for the areas to be overlapped. Refer to Stitching Techniques (page 22).

5 Cut a small rectangle from the chosen pocket fabric, about 7 × 6cm (2¾ × 2¼in), press under all the edges 6mm (¼in). Straight stitch one of the longer edges. Pin the pocket in place on the dress, stitched edge at the top, straight stitch to the dress around the remaining three sides.

6 Tack (baste), then appliqué the dress in place except for the areas to be overlapped. Refer to Stitching Techniques (page 22).

7 Apply teddy's head.

8 Machine straight stitch the detail on the arms, feet and ears (see worksheet right).

9 Hand embroider in straight stitch the eyes, nose and mouth using black embroidery thread (see worksheet right).

10 Cover the piping cord and complete the cushion back as described in Finishing (pages 26–7).

SIMPLY FLORAL
CUSHION

There are flowers in glorious simplicity on this vibrant yet easy-to-make cushion. Although there are few shapes to appliqué, the bold colours, four borders and piping create an eye-catching piece of work. The vase is an irregular shape, whilst French knots are stitched at random in the flower centres, implying a freedom from the conventional and expected image.

FINISHED SIZE: *38 × 38cm (15 × 15in)*

♥   50cm (½yd) fabric, 115cm (45in) wide, for the base/background and backing
♥   Four 15cm (6in) lengths appliqué fabric, 115cm (45in) wide, for the flowers, leaves, border strips and piping
♥   10cm (4in) lightweight checked fabric, 115cm (45in) wide, for one border
♥   Scraps of appliqué fabric for the flower centres and vase
♥   Threads to match the appliqué fabrics
♥   Embroidery thread for flower centres
♥   1.75m (2yd) piping cord
♥   38cm (15in) square cushion pad

1   Prepare your fabrics as described in Pre-stitching Preparation (page 17).

2   Cut out a 28cm (11in) square from the base/background fabric. Tack (baste) the outline of a 24cm (9½in) square onto the fabric, appliqué within it.

3   Cut out all the appliqué shapes using the templates on page 102.

4   Apply the vase first, except for the areas to be overlapped. Refer to Stitching Techniques (page 22). Stitch the flowers and leaves in place referring to the worksheet (right). Lastly apply the flower centres.

5   Embroider the French knots at random onto the flower centres.

6   Stitch the four borders around the appliqué using the method described in Finishing (wallhanging borders page 24.) The finished width of the inner and outer borders is 12mm (½in), the finished width of the two middle borders is 2.5cm (1in). The inner border strips are the shortest in length, the outer strips the longest.

7   Cover the piping cord and complete the cushion back as described in Finishing (pages 26–7).

♥ flowers are created in an abundance of different shapes & colours ◦ stitch French knots in the flower centres ♥

flower

piping

border

leaves

borders

background/backing flower borders

flowers

◦ flower centres ◦

vase

49

Alphabetical Cushions, Partly Patchwork
Cushion, Tabitha Teddy Cushion and
Moonstruck Mice Cushion

MOONSTRUCK MICE
CUSHION

The moon and stars are perennial motif favourites, and combined with any letter and simple animal shapes, numerous design ideas are possible. This easy-to-make cushion uses a dark starry background fabric to enhance and frame all the brightly coloured shapes.

FINISHED SIZE: *38 × 38cm (15 × 15in)*

♥   50cm (½yd) lightweight cotton fabric, 115cm (45in) wide, for the background and backing

♥   50cm (19in) square lightweight calico (muslin), for the base

♥   Three 25cm (10in) squares appliqué fabric, for the moon, letter and mice

♥   Scraps of appliqué fabric, for the stars

♥   25cm (¼yd) lightweight cotton fabric, 115cm (45in) wide, for the piping

♥   Narrow ribbon, for the tails

♥   Threads to match the appliqué fabrics

♥   1.75m (2yd) piping cord

♥   38cm (15in) square cushion pad

1   Prepare your fabrics as described in Pre-stitching Preparation (page 17).

2   Cut out all the appliqué shapes using the templates on page 103. The moon is the same as in the Summer Twilight Wallhanging (template on page 100).

3   Cut out a 50cm (19in) square from the background fabric and lay on top of the calico

(muslin). Tack (baste) the two firmly together to form a firm base. Refer to Fabrics (page 14).

4   Tack (baste) the mice in place, sliding the ends of the tail ribbons under the bodies. Leaving the nose of the mouse which is under the letter unstitched, and leaving the areas to be overlapped, refer to Stitching Techniques (page 22), satin stitch around the mice.

5   Gently fold the nose back over the mouse's body and position the letter so that the nose will lay over it when folded back (see worksheet right). Satin stitch in place. Fold the nose back over the letter, and, rejoining the line of satin stitch, apply the nose. Either embroider the eyes or stitch on tiny black beads. Straight stitch the whiskers.

6   Apply the stars and moon.

7   Cover the piping cord and complete the cushion back as described in Finishing (pages 26–7).

° eyes are beads or embroidered °

° tails are ribbon ° beware the cat! °

38 x 38 cm (15x15in)

background

stars

m

mice

° the moon is off - white °

backing

piping

BAG OF FRUIT
· · · · · · · · · · · · · · ·

Create a stir shopping with this striking bag, which is decorated with apples, pears and a hand reaching in on both sides. The fruit colours are vividly effective against the black and cream backgrounds. When you have learnt the technique, you can make bags of all sizes, colours and designs.

FINISHED SIZE: *34 × 37cm (13½ × 14½in)*

♥   50cm (½yd) lightweight calico (muslin), 115cm (45in) wide, for the base

♥   Two 50cm (½yd) lengths appliqué fabric, 115cm (45in) wide, for the hands and backgrounds (form the bag sides)

♥   Two 25cm (¼yd) lengths appliqué fabric, 115cm (45in) wide, for apples, pears and handles

♥   50cm (½yd) lightweight polyester wadding (batting), 115cm (45in) wide

♥   50cm (½yd) lightweight cotton fabric, 115cm (45in) wide, for the bag lining

♥   Threads to match the appliqué fabrics

1   Prepare your fabrics as described in Pre-stitching Preparation (page 17).

2   Cut two pieces of calico (muslin) 38 × 41cm (15 × 16in). Cut a 38 × 41cm (15 × 16in) piece from each of the two background fabrics. Tack (baste) together one piece of calico (muslin) and one of the background fabrics. Refer to Fabrics (page 14). Repeat with the two remaining pieces of fabric. These form the two bag sides.

3   Cut out all appliqué shapes using the templates on page 104. Tack (baste), then appliqué shapes in place on the bag sides, except for overlapping areas (refer to Stitching Techniques page 22). The black hand is applied to the cream background, and vice versa. When stitching, pivot the fabric

to ease the satin stitching evenly around the finger tops, refer to Stitching Techniques (page 21). The fruit stalks are satin stitched.

4   Cut two pieces of wadding (batting) the same size as the bag sides. Lay a piece of wadding over the wrong side of each bag side. Tack (baste) together. With the right side of each bag side facing inwards, pin the two sides together. The wadding (batting) will now be on the outside. Stitch together the bag sides and bottom, 12mm (½in) in from the edge, through all the layers. Turn out so that the right sides are outside, with the wadding inside. Remove tacking (basting).

5   For the handles cut two strips 47cm (18½in) long × 13cm (5in) wide, to give a finished size 44cm (17¼in) long x 5cm (2in) wide. Insert wadding (batting) in the centre of the handles. Make and attach handles and lining completing the bag as described in Finishing (pages 27–8).

34 x 37cm (13½ x 14½ in)

· simple colours are effective & striking · make shopping fun ·

lining

background

hand

background   hand   pears   apples

♥ wadding (batting) used to pad the bag & handles
♥ length of handles 44cm (17in)
♥ stalks satin stitched

55

SLEEPY TEDDY COT QUILT

Young children will love to snuggle under this colourful, cozy quilt! It can be made in colours to match or complement the Tabitha Teddy Cushion (page 46), and together they will create an appealing focus in a nursery. Easy patchwork and basic quiltmaking are included in this project.

FINISHED SIZE: 76 × 102cm (30 × 40in)

1.5m (1½yd) lightweight calico (muslin), 115cm (45in) wide, for the base/background and quilt backing

75cm (¾yd) appliqué fabric, 115cm (45in) wide, for the wide border

25cm (¼yd) appliqué fabric, 115cm (45in) wide, for the narrow border and patchwork

25cm (¼yd) appliqué fabric, 115cm (45in) wide, for the binding

50cm (19in) square appliqué fabric, for the pillow and patchwork

50cm (19in) square appliqué fabric, for teddy

Scraps of appliqué fabric, for the paw, ear and nightcap bobble

23cm (9in) square appliqué fabric, for nightcap

Five 15cm (6in) lengths appliqué fabric, 115cm (45in) wide, for patchwork

1m (1yd) lightweight polyester wadding (batting), 115cm (45in) wide

Tissue paper

Threads to match the appliqué fabrics

Black embroidery thread

1 Prepare your fabrics as described in Pre-stitching Preparation (page 17).

2 Cut a piece of calico (muslin) 44 x 69cm (17½ × 27¼in) for the central appliqué panel, which includes a seam allowance of 2cm (¾in) on each side. Cut four wide border strips 77.5cm (30½in) long x 16.5cm (6½in) wide, to give a finished width of 15cm (6in). Cut four narrow border strips 76cm (30in) long x 4cm (1½in) wide.

3 Cut sixteen 11.5cm (4½in) squares for the patchwork. The patchwork fabric does not need to be backed with vilene (pellon). Cut out the heart using the template on page 105. Tack (baste) tissue paper behind one of the squares. Appliqué

the heart to this square, tearing the tissue paper away from the back after stitching. Arrange the squares in four rows of four. Stitch each set of four squares together using a 6mm (¼in) seam, forming four separate stitched rows.

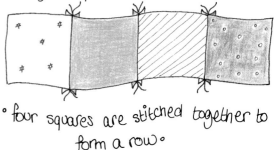

• four squares are stitched together to form a row •

Stitch together the four rows, matching the seamlines, to form teddy's quilt.

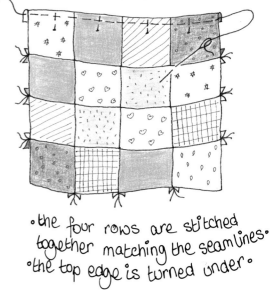

• the four rows are stitched together matching the seamlines •
• the top edge is turned under •

Turn under the top of the quilt 6mm (¼in) and tack (baste). The finished width should be the same as the calico (muslin) background piece.

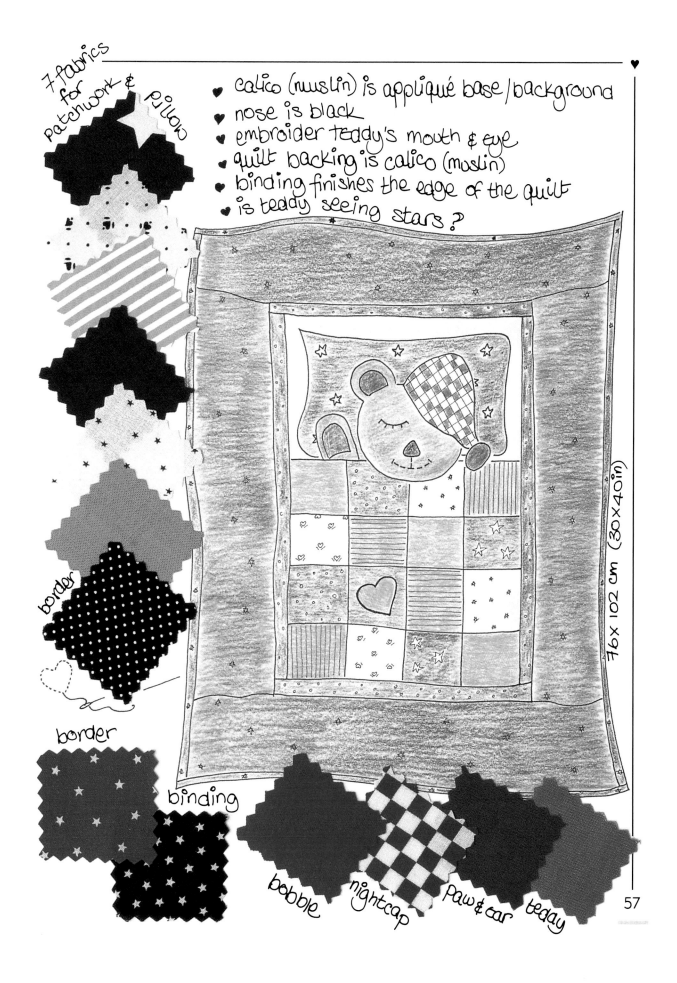

7 fabrics for patchwork & pillow

- ♥ calico (muslin) is appliqué base/background
- ♥ nose is black
- ♥ embroider teddy's mouth & eye
- ♥ quilt backing is calico (muslin)
- ♥ binding finishes the edge of the quilt
- ♥ is teddy seeing stars?

border

border

binding

bobble   nightcap   paw & ear   teday

76x 102 cm (30x40in)

57

4 Draw the pillow freehand, on the back of the fabric, cut out. Cut out all the appliqué shapes, using the templates on page 105. Satin stitch the pillow in place, except for the areas to be overlapped, refer to Stitching Techniques (page 22). Appliqué the two paw pieces in position, leaving the bottom edge of the larger piece unstitched.

5 With the folded edge at the top, place teddy's quilt onto the calico (muslin) just below the pillow, covering the raw edge of the paw, and level with the bottom and side raw edges of the calico (muslin). Criss cross with tacking (basting) to hold firmly in place. Machine straight stitch the top edge of the quilt to the calico (muslin).

6 Appliqué teddy's head in position (see worksheet page 57). Add the dark ear patch, nightcap, bobble and nose. Hand embroider the mouth and eye (see worksheet) using black embroidery thread.

7 Stitch the narrow border in place using the method described in Finishing (wallhanging borders, page 24). Add the wide border in the same way.

8 Cut pieces of wadding (batting) and calico (muslin) the same size as the completed quilt top. Lay the calico (muslin), wadding (batting) and quilt top, right side up, on top of each other so that the wadding (batting) is sandwiched between the other two. Criss cross with tacking (basting) to hold the three layers securely together.

9 Cut four 4cm (1½in) wide strips of binding fabric, two the length of the quilt and two the width, plus 8cm (3in) extra on each strip. Bind the two long sides of the quilt first. Place a binding strip along one edge of the quilt, right sides and raw edges together, machine straight stitch in place 6mm (¼in) in from the edges.

stitch binding along the edge of the quilt, right sides together.

Fold the binding over the raw edge, turn under a 6mm (¼in) hem and pin to the back of the quilt, just covering the line of stitching.

2. stitch this binding across the binding already in place.

1. turning under a 6mm (¼in) hem, slip stitch the binding down. trim off the excess fabric at the corner.

° fold the excess fabric inwards around the corner.

° fold the binding over at the top.

° fold the binding down over the corner, concealing all the raw edges.

Slip stitch all along this hemline. Cut off excess fabric at each end. Repeat for the second side. Bind the top and bottom edges of the quilt, covering the binding already in place, at the corners. Proceed as before, but to finish off the corners turn the excess fabric inwards (see drawings on this page) before slip stitching.

FLYING KITES WALLHANGING

Kites are made in gorgeous, vibrant colours and a visit to a kitemaker's workshop or just watching kites fly in the blue sky, is a feast for the eyes. In this project there is plenty of practice at stitching points, one of the more difficult techniques to perfect. The border is stitched in place before the work is finished so that the sleeves can be stitched over the border.

FINISHED SIZE: *65 × 29cm (25½ × 11½in)*

♥ 50cm (½yd) appliqué fabric, 115cm (45in) wide, for sky background

♥ 50 cm (½yd) lightweight wadding (batting), 115cm (45in) wide, for the base

♥ 50cm (½yd) Indian Madras cotton, 115cm (45in) wide, for the backing, border, casing and one cuff

♥ Eight 25cm (10in) squares appliqué fabric, for the clouds, kites, mittens, sleeves and one cuff

♥ Threads to match the appliqué fabrics

♥ Rod and cord for hanging

1 Prepare your fabrics as described in Pre-stitching Preparation (page 17).

2 Cut out the background fabric and wadding (batting) to the required size, and firmly tack (baste) together.

3 Cut out all the appliqué shapes using the templates on page 106. Although each kite has two colours, cut a whole kite shape from one of them and the two diagonally opposed triangles in the contrasting colour (see drawing below).

4 Appliqué the clouds in place.

5 Cut four 4cm (1½in) wide border strips, to give a finished width of 2.5cm (1in), two the length of the wallhanging and two the width, plus 8cm (3in) extra on each strip. Stitch the borders in place using the method described in Finishing (wallhanging borders page 24). Place the strips, right sides together, 2.5cm (1in) in from the edge, along seamline. When the border is complete, secure it in place by tacking (basting) around the raw edges of the work, through all the layers.

6 Apply the whole kite shapes to the background first, straight stitching the edges to be covered by the triangles. Position the triangles on top, then satin stitch in place. Apply the mittens, except for the areas to be overlapped (see page 22), then the sleeves, stitching over the borders, then the cuffs.

7 Topstitch (see worksheet right) the kite strings and mitten details.

8 From remaining fabric scraps cut out the tail bows, tack (baste) in position, then satin stitch.

9 Follow the procedure described in Finishing (page 24) to cut out and complete the backing and casing.

10 Thread the rod through the casing and attach the cord.

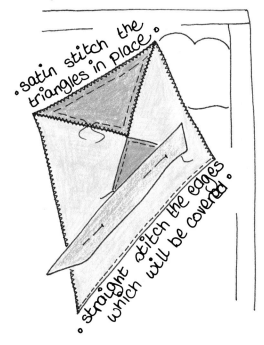

satin stitch the triangles in place

straight stitch the edges which will be covered

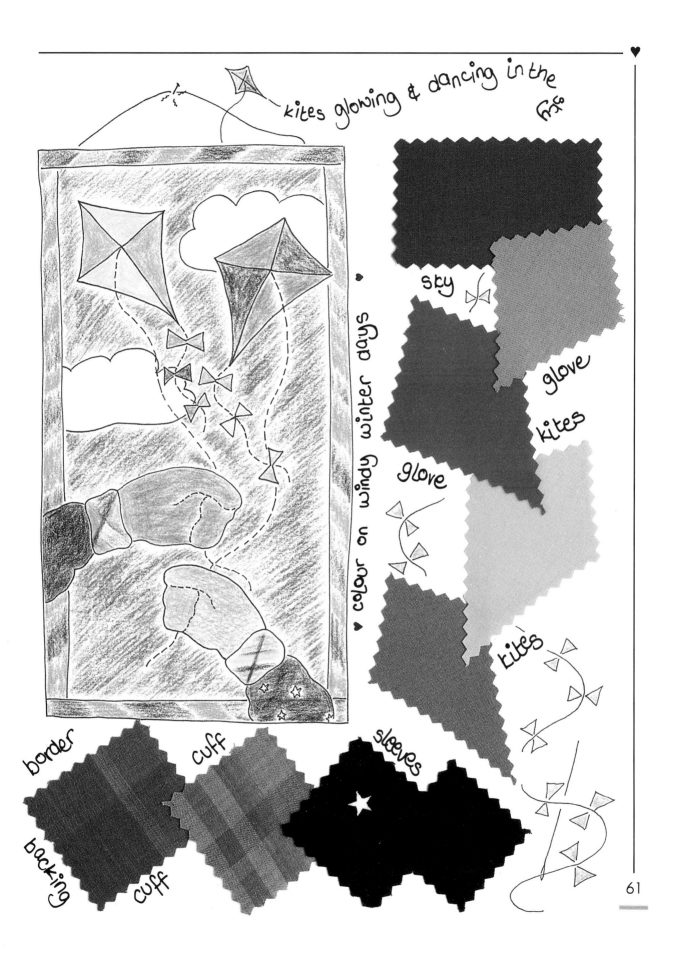

kites glowing & dancing in the sky

♥ colour on windy winter days •

sky

glove

kites

glove

kites

border

backing

cuff

cuff

sleeves

RAINY DAY CHILD'S BAG

Children love their own little bags, particularly if made-to-measure for them. A sturdy, black fabric has been chosen as the base for this project, making a perfect foil for the rainbow-coloured appliqué.

FINISHED SIZE: 23 × 25cm (9 × 10in)

♥   50cm (½yd) medium-weight cotton, 115cm (45in) wide, for the base/background and handles
♥   50cm (½yd) appliqué fabric, 115cm (45in) wide, for the lining, handle lining and umbrella
♥   30cm (12in) square white appliqué fabric, for the duck
♥   Scraps of appliqué fabric, for puddles, raindrops, duck's beak and feet, boots and umbrella
♥   Threads to match the appliqué fabrics
♥   Black embroidery thread

1   Prepare your fabrics as described in Pre-stitching Preparation (page 17).

2   Cut two bag sides from the base/background cotton 25 × 28cm (10 × 11in), including a 12mm (½in) seam allowance. Draw the puddles freehand on the back of the fabric, cut out. Cut out all the appliqué shapes using the templates on page 107. Cut the two outer panels of the umbrella with an extra 3mm (⅛in) on the inside edges.

3   Apply puddles and raindrops to each side of the bag, except for areas to be overlapped, see Stitching Techniques (page 22). On one side of the bag, position the duck's beak and feet, satin stitch in place. Apply the duck's body. On the other side of the bag, apply the boots first, then the umbrella. Position the two outer panels of the umbrella, tack (baste) then satin stitch in place — except for the inside edges. Position the centre panel (trim fabric from the outer panels if necessary), to cover the two raw edges. Tack (baste) then satin stitch right around panel.

4   Straight stitch the rain and embroider the duck's eye by hand (see worksheet right).

5   For the bag handles, cut two strips of base fabric and two of lining fabric each 4 × 40cm (1½ × 15½in) to make handles with a finished size of 2.5 × 38cm (1 × 15in). With right sides together, stitch one strip of base fabric to one strip of lining fabric, down both long sides, leaving the ends open. Pull through so right sides are outside, press.

6   Make and attach the lining and bag handles and complete the bag as described in Finishing (pages 27–8).

- duck is white
- eye is embroidered
- rain is machine straight stitched

bag & handles

raindrops

puddles

umbrellas are made in such fabulous colours

boots

duck's feet & beak

umbrella • lining • umbrella

BREAKFAST TIME
PLACEMATS

Start the day with a smile using these fun, colourful placemats, suitable for adults and children alike. Appliqué a favourite food onto the plates, and add a personal touch by applying an initial on the mugs. The mats have wadding (batting) inside them to protect the table from hot dishes. As the appliqué design has lots of small pieces you may find it fiddly to complete.

FINISHED SIZE: *38 × 47cm (15 × 18½in)*

For two placemats you will need:
♥ 1m (1yd) lightweight cotton, 115cm (45in) wide, for the base/background and backing
♥ 50cm (½yd) lightweight polyester wadding (batting), 115cm (45in) wide
♥ 25cm (10in) appliqué fabric, 115cm (45in) wide for the plates and mugs
♥ 25cm (10in) appliqué fabric, 115cm (45in) wide for the plates, letters and binding
♥ 10cm (4in) appliqué fabric, 115cm (45in) wide, for the knives, fork and spoon
♥   0cm (4in) appliqué fabric, 115cm (45in) wide, for the mice and egg
♥ Scraps of appliqué fabric for the toast, egg cup, egg whites, yolk and sausage
♥ Tissue paper
♥ Threads to match the appliqué fabrics
♥ Black embroidery thread

1   Prepare your fabrics as described in Pre-stitching Preparation (page 17).

2   Cut the base/background cotton and wadding (batting) for the two mats, to the finished size. Tack (baste) the base/background and wadding (batting), for each mat, securely together.

3   Cut out all the appliqué shapes using the templates on page 108. The mice are the same as

in the Moonstruck Mice Cushion (template on page 103), but reduced to 10.5cm (4¼in) body length. Draw the toast, sausage and letters freehand, on the back of the fabrics, cut out.

4   Tack (baste) tissue paper onto the back of the mugs, appliqué the initials in place. Tear away the tissue paper. Satin stitch the mugs in place on the mats.

5   Tack (baste) the centre of the plates in place on the background fabric. Place the outer ring of the plate over this and tack (baste) securely. Satin stitch around the inner and outer edges, except for the areas to be overlapped, refer to Stitching Techniques (page 22).

6   Apply the knives, fork and spoon. Next the pieces of toast, the eggs, egg cup and sausage.

7   Lastly, satin stitch the mice in place. The tails are satin stitched, the whiskers straight stitched and the eyes embroidered by hand (see worksheet right).

8   Cut the backing fabric to the same size as the mats. Tack (baste) all the layers together. Bind the edges, following the instructions given for the Sleepy Teddy Cot Quilt (pages 56–9).

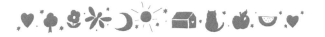

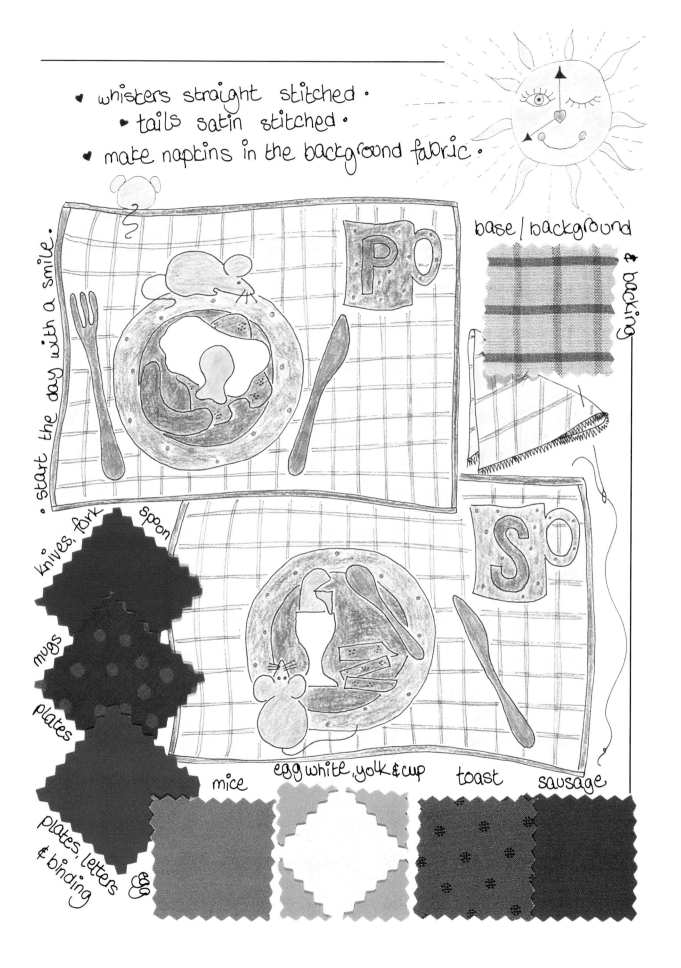

FRESH FLOWERS
WALLHANGING

Capture the essence of spring with this eyecatching wallhanging, which will brighten up the darkest of rooms. Combine fresh spring colours, evocative of a new season on its way, with softer more muted colours to give a bright effect. Alternatively choose warmer, autumnal shades for a glowing result that will look just as effective. Accuracy will be needed when applying the flowers stems as they all need to fit into the jug.

FINISHED SIZE: *43 × 49cm (17 × 19¼in)*

♥   75cm (¾yd) light- or medium-weight cotton fabric, 115cm (45in) wide, for the base/ background, backing and casing

♥   50cm (½yd) lightweight calico (muslin) 115cm (45in) wide, for the base, optional

♥   23cm (9in) square appliqué fabric, for the jug

♥   Four 10cm (4in) lengths appliqué fabric, 115cm (45in) wide for the flowers, stems and leaves

♥   15cm (6in) appliqué fabric, 115cm (45in) wide, for the stems and border

♥   Scraps of appliqué fabric, for the flower centres

♥   Threads to match the appliqué fabrics

♥   Rod and cord for hanging

1   Prepare your fabrics as described in Pre-stitching Preparation (page 17).

2   Cut the base/background fabric to 44.5 × 50.5cm (17½ × 19¾in), including a 12mm (½in) seam allowance. Use calico (muslin) behind the background fabric, if necessary, to create a firm base for the appliqué.

3   Cut four 4cm (1½in) wide border strips to give a finished width of 2.5cm (1in), two the length of the wallhanging and two the width, plus 8cm (3in) extra on each strip. Stitch the border in place using the method described in Finishing (page 24).

4   Cut out all the appliqué shapes using the templates on page 109. Use the flower templates, slightly enlarged, from the Simply Floral Wallhanging (page 102), in addition to the templates for this project. Draw the stems freehand on the back of the fabric, except the stem with the leaf, and cut out.

5   Tack (baste) in place all the leaves, flowers and stems which touch no other shapes (see worksheet right). Satin stitch in place. Build up the picture, shape by shape, first tacking (basting) then satin stitching in place, except for the areas to be overlapped, refer to Stitching Techniques (page 22). Keep checking that the stems fit into the top of the jug, by holding the jug shape over them. The stem that curves down over the jug is laid in place, but satin stitched after the jug has been applied. When the flowers are all in place, apply their centres.

6   Fold the curved stem away from the jug and apply the jug, stitching over all the stems. Fold the curved stem back and satin stitch this and its flower to finish the appliqué.

7   Follow the procedure described in Finishing (page 24) to cut out and complete the backing and casing.

8   Thread the rod through the casing and attach the cord.

Size 43 × 49 cm (17 × 19¼ in) • lovely fresh colours •

• capture the essence of fresh spring flowers •

• flowers •

• Jug •

• stems • border & leaves •

• backing •

• background

• flower centres • white too •

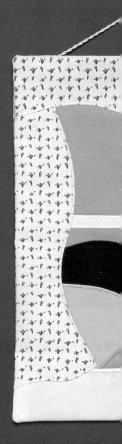

(clockwise from top left)
Summer Twilight Wallhanging,
Summer View Wallhanging,
Sunny Window Wallhanging,
Happy Hearts Wallhangings,
Apple Harvest Wallhanging

HOME-MADE APRON

Fruit and vegetables, with their different shapes, sizes and colours, look wonderful grouped together. This project is easy to complete, especially if you use a ready-made apron, though you could make your own in a soft, sturdy ticking (pillow ticking). Adapt the idea for a child's or gardener's apron using appropriate appliqué decorations.

FINISHED SIZE (excluding tapes): 93 × 65cm (36½ × 25½in)

♥ Apron – home-made or bought ready-made
♥ 25cm (¼yd) appliqué fabric, 115cm (45in) wide for the spoons
♥ Scraps of appliqué fabric in thirteen different colours, for the fruit, vegetables, leaves and stalks (see worksheet right)
♥ Embroidery threads for the seeds
♥ Threads to match the appliqué fabrics

1 Prepare your fabrics as described in Pre-stitching Preparation (page 17).

2 Cut out all the shapes using the templates on pages 110–11. The apple and pear are from the Bag of Fruit, templates on page 104, enlarged slightly.

3 Apply the spoons by tucking the spoon handles into the pocket, tack (baste) then satin stitch holding the pocket clear.

4 Hand embroider the melon and strawberry seeds before applying the shapes to the apron. Tack (baste) then satin stitch all the shapes in place, except for the areas to be overlapped, refer to Stitching Techniques (page 22). The pink part of the melon and the pepper stalk are applied before the green skin of the melon and the pepper. The tomato, strawberry and aubergine are all applied before their stalks.

5 Complete by satin stitching the apple and pear stalks and carrot leaves, finishing off as neatly as possible on the back of the apron as it will not be hidden!

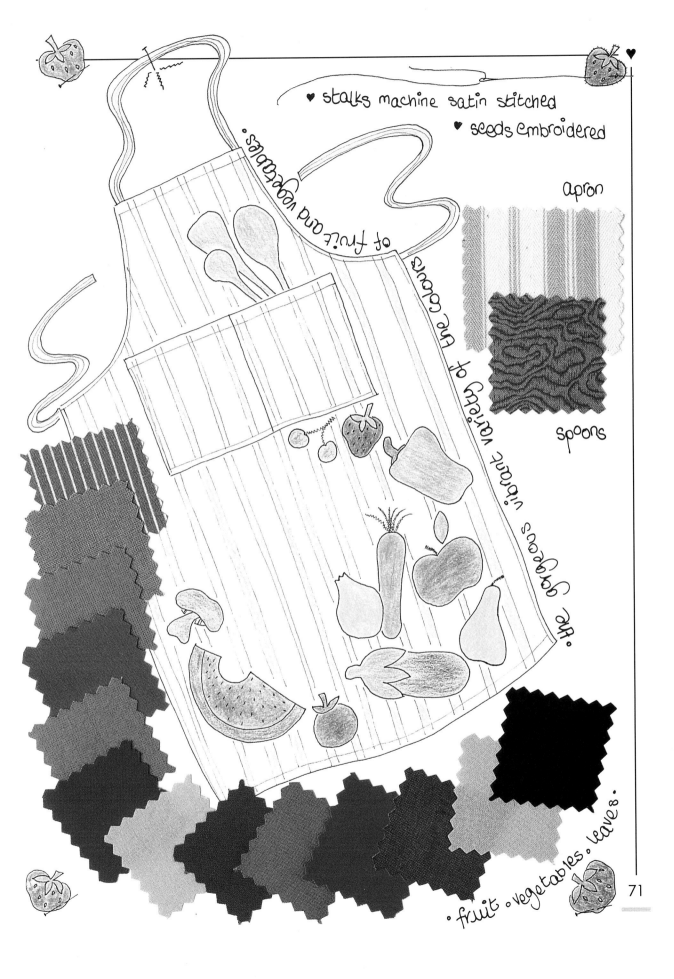

♥ stalks machine satin stitched
♥ seeds embroidered

apron

of fruit and vegetables

the colours of the

gorgeous vibrant variety

spoons

the gorgeous

• fruit • vegetables • leaves •

71

SUN, SEA AND SAND BAG

Carry all you need for a day at the beach in this sunny, capacious bag, made in tropical, seaside colours. All the shapes are stitched through both the background fabric and the wadding. Wavy lines, suggesting movement, are straight stitched across the sea on the beach side of the bag, whilst the sun's rays, also straight stitched, effectively and simply machine quilt the sunny side of the bag. Though easy to make, the thin piping around the bag gives it a professional finish.

FINISHED SIZE: 48 × 38cm (19 × 15in)

♥ 75cm (¾yd) lightweight cotton fabric, 115cm (45in) wide, for the background (which forms the bag sides) and handles

♥ 75cm (¾yd) lightweight cotton wadding (batting), 115cm (45in) wide

♥ Four 10cm (4in) lengths appliqué fabric, 115cm (45in) wide, for the sea and palm leaves

♥ 25cm (¼yd) appliqué fabric, 115cm (45in) wide, for the sand

♥ Two 30cm (12in) squares appliqué fabric for the towel and sun

♥ Scraps of appliqué fabric, for the hat, hatband, sails and boat

♥ 50cm (½yd) lightweight cotton fabric, 115cm (45in) wide, for the lining and piping

♥ Threads to match the appliqué fabrics

♥ 1.5m (1½yd) thin piping cord

1 Prepare your fabrics as described in Pre-stitching Preparation (page 17).

2 Cut two bag sides and two pieces of wadding (batting) 50.5 × 40.5cm (20 × 16in), including a 12mm (½in) seam allowance. Tack together firmly the background fabric and wadding.

3 Cut out all the appliqué shapes using the templates on page 112. Draw the sun, sea, sand and towel pieces freehand, on the back of the fabrics, cut out. The large sun rays are triangles.

4 Apply the triangular sun rays, except for the areas to be overlapped, refer to Stitching Techniques (page 22). Apply the sun. Straight stitch the sun's rays in random lengths, through the background and wadding.

5 Apply the layers of the sea and sand. Straight stitch wavy lines onto the sea. Apply the boat and sails, the towel, hat and hatband. Satin stitch the palm leaves in place.

6 Cover the piping cord and tack (baste) to the two sides and base of the bag as described in Finishing (page 26, piping a cushion). Stitch the two sides together.

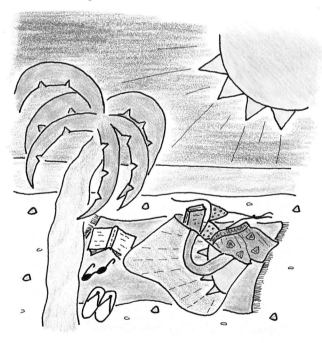

7 For the handles cut two strips 47cm (18½in) long × 13cm (5in) wide, to give a finished size 44cm (17¼in) long × 5cm (2in) wide. Make and attach the handles and lining and complete the bag as described in Finishing (pages 27–8).

piping

lining

towel

hat

hat band

sails

boat

background

sand

sea

handles

? fish • shells • • shark's fin • swimsuit • next time !

size : 46 × 38 cm (19 × 15 in)

leaves

sun

♥ wadding (batting) inside the handles •

♥ could make handles longer to go over the shoulder?

♥ simple machine quilting creates the sun's rays •

CHRISTMAS TABLE MAT

Suitably festive, this mat will look beautiful in the centre of the table. Easy-to-make as a gift, or use the method to make individual placemats. Choose bright reds and greens for the Christmas motifs and use cotton fabric which is already quilted, or machine quilt some calico (muslin) yourself. The base/background needs a backing – consider a Christmas print – and binding.

FINISHED SIZE: *63.5 × 46cm (25 × 18in)*

♥ 75cm (¾yd) ready-quilted cotton fabric, 115cm (45in) wide, for the base/background

♥ 25cm (¼yd) appliqué fabric, 115cm (45in) wide, for the leaves and binding

♥ Four 10cm (4in) lengths appliqué fabric, 115cm (45in) wide, for the holly leaves, leaves and apple

♥ Two 10cm (4in) lengths appliqué fabric, 115cm (45in) wide, for apples, berries and hearts

♥ Threads to match the appliqué fabrics

♥ 75cm (¾yd) light- or medium-weight calico (muslin), 115cm (45in) wide, for the backing

1 Prepare your fabrics as described in Pre-stitching Preparation (page 17).

2 Cut a rectangle of the base/background fabric 63.5 × 46cm (25 × 18in). Cut each corner in a curve to create the mat's oval shape (see worksheet right).

3 Cut out all appliqué shapes using templates on page 109. The heart is the same as in Sleepy Teddy Quilt, enlarged slightly (template page 105). The apples are the same as in Summer Twilight and Bag of Fruit (template pages 100 and 104).

4 Tack (baste) and satin stitch the shapes in place (see worksheet right), except for overlapping areas, refer to Stitching Techniques (page 22). To ease the stitching around the berries, pivot several times, refer to Stitching Techniques (page 21).

5 The detail on the holly leaves and the apple stalks are satin stitched (see worksheet right).

6 Cut the backing fabric the same size as the mat. Tack (baste) the layers together. Bind the edges following the instructions given for the Sleepy Teddy Cot Quilt (pages 56–9).

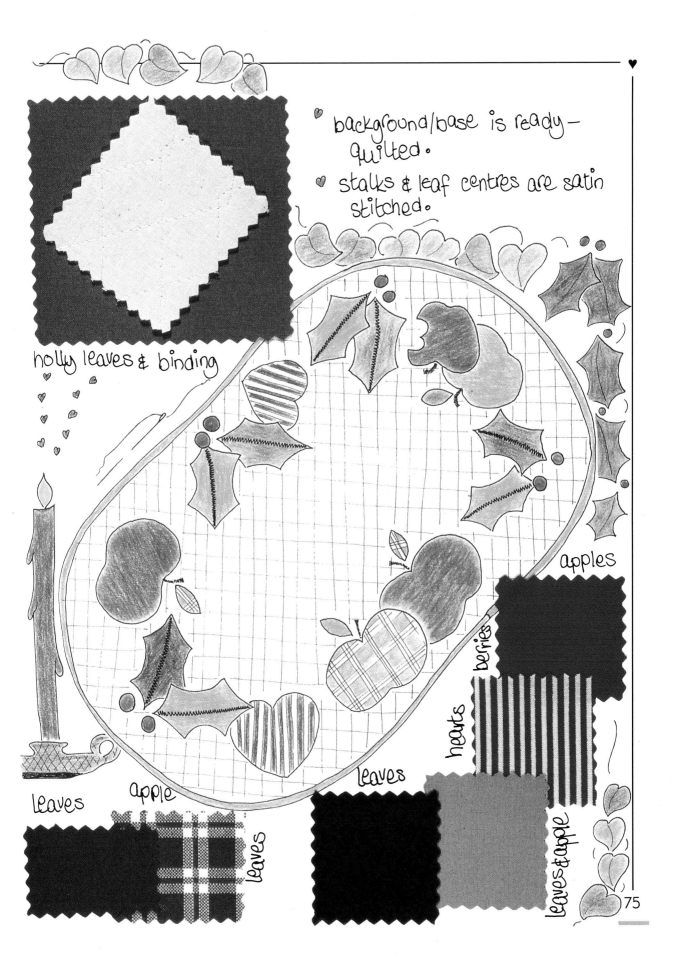

- background/base is ready-quilted.
- stalks & leaf centres are satin stitched.

holly leaves & binding

apples

berries

hearts

leaves

leaves

apple

leaves

leaves&apple

FLOWERS FOR YOU
CUSHION

Boldly coloured shapes on a pale background will always make an impression, as shown by this stunning floral cushion. The colours enhance the border fabric whilst an inner row of piping outlines the appliqué design. The cover uses the same flowers as in the Simply Floral Cushion (pages 48–9) and Fresh Flowers Wallhanging (pages 66–7), and shows how a different look can be achieved by changing colours and positions. Easy to make, the only fiddly part is applying the ribbon tie.

FINISHED SIZE: *38 × 38cm (15 × 15in)*

♥ 46cm (18in) square base/background fabric
♥ 50cm (½yd) light-medium-weight cotton fabric, 115cm (45in) wide, for the border and backing
♥ Three 10cm (4in) lengths appliqué fabric, 115cm (45in) wide, for the flowers, piping, stalks and leaves
♥ Scraps of appliqué fabrics in five different colours, for the flower centres, flowers and leaves
♥ Narrow ribbon
♥ Threads to match the appliqué fabrics
♥ 4.5m (5yd) piping cord
♥ 38cm (15in) square cushion pad

1 Prepare your fabrics as described in Pre-stitching Preparation (page 17).

2 Cut out a 32.5cm (12½in) square from the base/background fabric. Tack (baste) the outline of a 30.5 (12in) square onto the fabric, work within it. Cut four border strips, 41m (16in) long × 5cm (2in) wide, to give a finished width of 4cm (1½in).

3 Cut out all the appliqué shapes using the templates for the flowers and leaves from the Simply Floral and Fresh Flowers projects (pages 102 and 109). Draw the stems freehand, on the back of the fabric, cut out.

4 Lay the ribbon forming the bouquet tie in place on the base/background fabric (see worksheet right), tack (baste) firmly, keeping the ends clear of the stitching. Satin stitch the stems in place, one by one, except for the areas to be overlapped. Refer to Stitching Techniques (page 22). Secure the ribbon at the same time, tie the bow over the stems.

5 Tack (baste) and satin stitch all the flowers and leaves in place.

6 Cover the piping cord, see Finishing (page 26), for the inner row of piping. This is applied in four separate lengths and stitched into the inner seamline of the border. Tack (baste) the top and bottom lengths around the completed appliqué. Next tack (baste) the two side lengths, covering both ends of the top and bottom lengths (see worksheet).

7 Stitch the borders around the appliqué, close up to and covering the raw edges of the piping, see Finishing (wallhanging borders, page 24, and cushion piping, page 26).

8 Cover the outer row of piping cord and complete the cushion back as described in Finishing (pages 26–7).

piping

piping & flowers

ribbon

base/background

borders & piping

leaves &

stems

leaves

flower centres

◦ 2 rows of piping ◦ ribbon around the bunch of flowers ◦

bunch of flowers ◦   ♥ for you ♥

◦ size 38 × 38 cm (15 × 15 in) ◦

SWEET DREAMS
HOT-WATER BOTTLE COVER

. . . .

Encase a hot-water bottle in this enchanting cover, the cosy answer to cold winter nights. Many winter and night-time images can be used for the appliqué, as well as initials, and it would make a fabulous Christmas gift. Buy the hot-water bottle first and make the cover, which features a large top opening for easy access, to fit. A more difficult project to complete.

♥ 50cm (½yd) ready-quilted cotton fabric, 115cm (45in) wide, for the base and back and extra padding
♥ Two 30cm (12in) lengths appliqué fabric, 115cm (45in) wide, for the backgrounds, piping and lining
♥ 10cm (4in) appliqué fabric, 115cm (45in) wide, for the sheep
♥ Scraps of appliqué fabric in four different colours, for the sheep's heads, legs and numbers
♥ Threads to match the appliqué fabrics
♥ 1m (1yd) piping cord
♥ Velcro
♥ Hot-water bottle

1 Prepare all your fabrics as described in Pre-stitching Preparation (page 17).

2 Make a paper template of your hot-water bottle, allowing a 6mm (¼in) seam all round. From the ready-quilted fabric, cut out the two cover pieces, extending the top of the front piece so that it is long enough to fold over the bottle and fasten on the other side (see drawings on page 80). Cut out the two background pieces. The appliqué is worked on the front of the cover only, the back remains plain.

3 Cut out the appliqué shapes using the templates on page 113.

4 Tack (baste) the two background fabrics onto the front of the cover, one overlapping the other, completely covering the base fabric. Satin stitch the overlapping piece in place.

5 Appliqué the numbers and sheep's legs in place, except for the areas to be overlapped, refer to Stitching Techniques (page 22), then their bodies and finally their heads. Add another layer of quilted fabric to the inside of the cover, if required.

6 Cover the piping cord and tack (baste) in place all round the appliquéd side of the cover, see Finishing (page 26), beginning and ending at the base (see drawing below).

7 Make a fabric loop, see Finishing (page 24), and tack (baste) to the base, between the two ends of the piping, raw edges outwards, the loop lying back along the cover (see drawing below).

8 To line the opening, cut two pieces from the sky background fabric: one piece the same shape

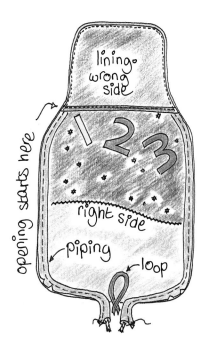

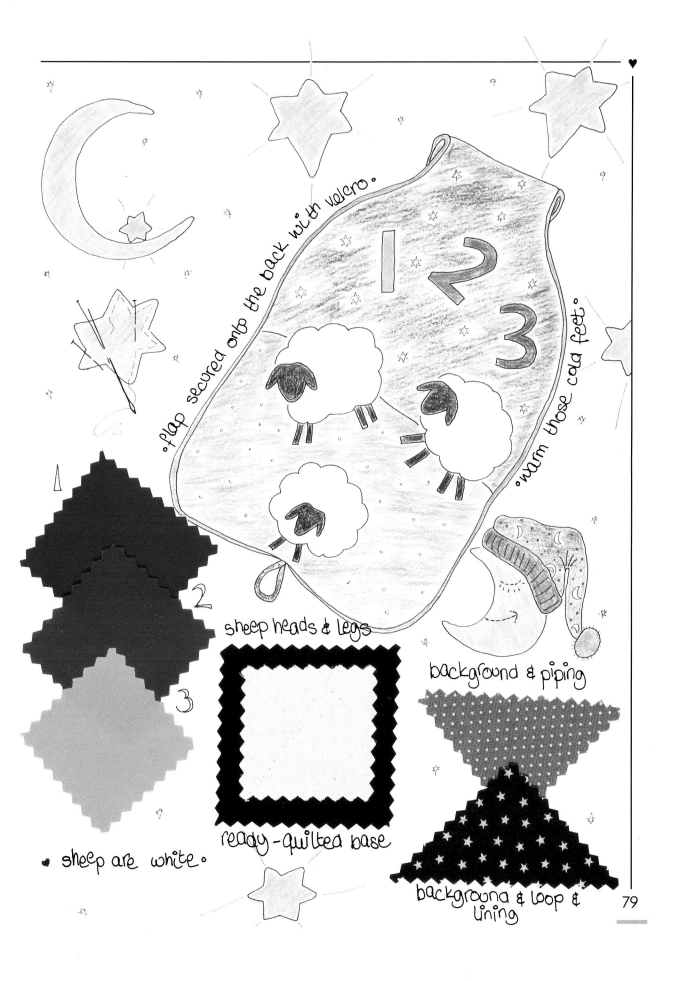

flap secured onto the back with velcro.

warm those cold feet.

sheep heads & legs

background & piping

ready-quilted base

• sheep are white.

background & loop & lining

as the top of the front, the other the same as the top of the back; both should be long enough to line the top of the cover down to the beginning of the opening. The opening starts where the cover begins to narrow. Stitch a narrow hem along the bottom edges of the linings (see drawings below). With right sides together, place these linings onto the corresponding sides of the cover, tack (baste) then machine straight stitch in place, at the same time securing the piping around the top edge of the front of the cover.

9 Leaving the linings inside out and with right sides together, tack (baste) the front and back of the cover together. Straight stitch along the seamline, from the opening edge round to the opening edge (see drawing below). Turn the cover and linings through to their right sides.

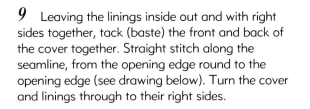

10 Stitch the velcro onto the top edge of each side, inside on the front and outside on the back of the cover. This holds the opening flap closed and conceals the top of the bottle.

(right) Wild Poppy Wallhanging

WILD POPPY
WALLHANGING

Poppies glow like jewels in the fields and along the roadsides, and their bright red petals viewed against golden fields and green grasses make a natural lesson in the observation of colour. This enchanting wallhanging would make a delightful gift for someone who loves wild flowers, or use the basic design to create several pictures depicting different wild flowers in celebration of the countryside. Use is made of wide satin stitches to create some of the detailing.

FINISHED SIZE: *41 × 22cm (16 × 8¾in)*

♥   30cm (12in) lightweight calico (muslin), 115cm (45in) wide, for the base and backing

♥   42cm (16½in) square appliqué fabric, for the sky

♥   10cm (4in) appliqué fabric, 115cm (45in) wide, for the grass and stem

♥   Scraps of appliqué fabric, for the stone wall, fence, fields and poppy centre

♥   10cm (4in) lightweight cotton, 115cm (45in) wide, for the borders and loops

♥   Threads to match the appliqué fabrics

♥   Black embroidery thread

♥   Rod and cord for hanging

1   Prepare your fabrics as described in Pre-stitching Preparation (page 17).

2   Cut a piece of the base calico (muslin) to 42 × 23cm (16½ × 9¼in), the finished size plus 6mm (¼in) seam allowance. Tack (baste) the background sky fabric to the calico (muslin).

3   Cut out all the appliqué shapes using the templates on page 114. Draw the fields, foreground grass and fence freehand on the back of the fabrics, cut out.

4   Tack (baste) then satin stitch the fields and grass in place onto the base/background fabric, except for the areas to be overlapped. Refer to Stitching Techniques (page 22). Apply the fence, then the stone wall shape.

5   Machine straight stitch a series of randomly placed straight lines, moving the work up and down under the needle, to create the grass detail (see worksheet right).

6   Tack (baste) the bud of the poppy in place, satin stitch. Tack (baste) the stem in place, satin stitch, easing the stitching carefully through all the small points of the leaf. Refer to Stitching Techniques (page 21). An extra row of wide, open satin stitch is machined along some parts of the stem and bud (see worksheet right) to suggest the tiny hairs on a poppy stem.

7   Apply the poppy flower, then the centre. The petal detail is satin stitched, the stamens are hand embroidered (see worksheet).

8   Cut the border strips 25mm (1in) wide, allowing 6mm (¼in) seams to give a finished border width of about 12mm (½in), two 43.5cm (17in) long and two 24.5cm (9¾in) long. Stitch on the borders as described in Finishing (page 24).

9   Make the loops and tack (baste) in place as described in Finishing (page 24).

10 Follow the procedure described in Finishing (page 24) to cut out and complete the backing.

11 Thread the rod through the loops and attach the cord.

border

sky

poppy

grass·stem

field

field

wall

fence

in celebration of all wild flowers in all lands.

· 41 × 22 cm (16 × 8¾ in) ·

💜 extra wide, open satin stitching on the stalk and bud, suggests hairs.

💜 grass detail machine straight stitched.

💜 hand embroidered stamens.

💜 backing is calico (muslin).

💜 rod natural wood · red cord.

💜 narrow borders · about 12mm (½in) finished size.

APPLE HARVEST
WALLHANGING

Trees, with their different outlines and colours, offer an ever-changing supply of images. And what could be more evocative than an apple tree in autumn? This wallhanging captures the spirit of harvest time, combining the colours of ripe apples and harvested fields with the simple shapes of rolling hills, all offset by the straight lines of the fence and ladder.

FINISHED SIZE: $42 \times 42cm$ ($16\frac{1}{2}in \times 16\frac{1}{2}in$)

♥ 46cm (18in) square lightweight polyester wadding (batting)

♥ 25cm (¼yd) appliqué fabric, 115cm (45in) wide, for the sky

♥ 30cm (12in) appliqué fabric 115cm (45in) wide, for the grass and leaves

♥ 25cm (¼yd) appliqué fabric, 115cm (45in) wide, for the tree foliage and hill

♥ Scraps of appliqué fabric, for the tree trunk, fence, ladder, hills, rug, basket and apples

♥ 46cm (18in) square lightweight cotton fabric, for the backing and casing

♥ Threads to match the appliqué fabrics

♥ Tissue paper

♥ Rod and cord for hanging

1 Prepare your fabrics as described in Pre-stitching Preparation (page 17).

2 Draw the sky and grass shapes freehand on the back of the fabrics, cut out. Tack (baste) the sky fabric onto the top half of the wadding (batting). Tack (baste) the grass fabric onto the wadding (batting), covering the bottom raw edge of the sky. The base wadding (batting) should be complete covered. Tack (baste) the outline of a 42cm (16½in) square onto the wallhanging, work within it.

3 Cut out all the appliqué shapes using the templates on page 115. Draw the fields, fence, ladder uprights and rungs, and rug freehand on the back of the fabrics, cut out. Cut out eleven apples and six leaves.

4 Undo some of the tacking (basting) holding the grass fabric, so that the four hilly fields can be applied, working from the top down. Replace the grass fabric, tack (baste) in position, satin stitch along its length, except for the areas to be overlapped. Refer to Stitching Techniques (page 22).

5 Tack (baste) and satin stitch the fence rails and posts. Apply the tree trunk and rug. The bottom edge of the rug is stitched into the seam.

6 Tack (baste) the fabric tree shape onto several layers of tissue paper. Satin stitch five apples with their stalks, and the leaves onto the fabric – a No 70(9) needle may be helpful for these shapes. Tear away the tissue paper. Tack (baste) the tree in place covering the tops of the branches. Satin stitch around the curved sides of the tree, the two straight sides will be stitched into the seam. Straight stitch some curved lines onto the tree (see worksheet right).

7 Tack (baste) the rungs of the ladder in place, satin stitch. Repeat for the ladder uprights.

8 Apply the apples at the base of the tree, then those in the basket. Satin stitch the stalks.

9 Finally, apply the basket so that only the top half of the apples are seen.

10 Follow the procedure described in Finishing (page 24) to cut out and complete the backing and casing.

11 Thread the rod through the casing and attach the cord.

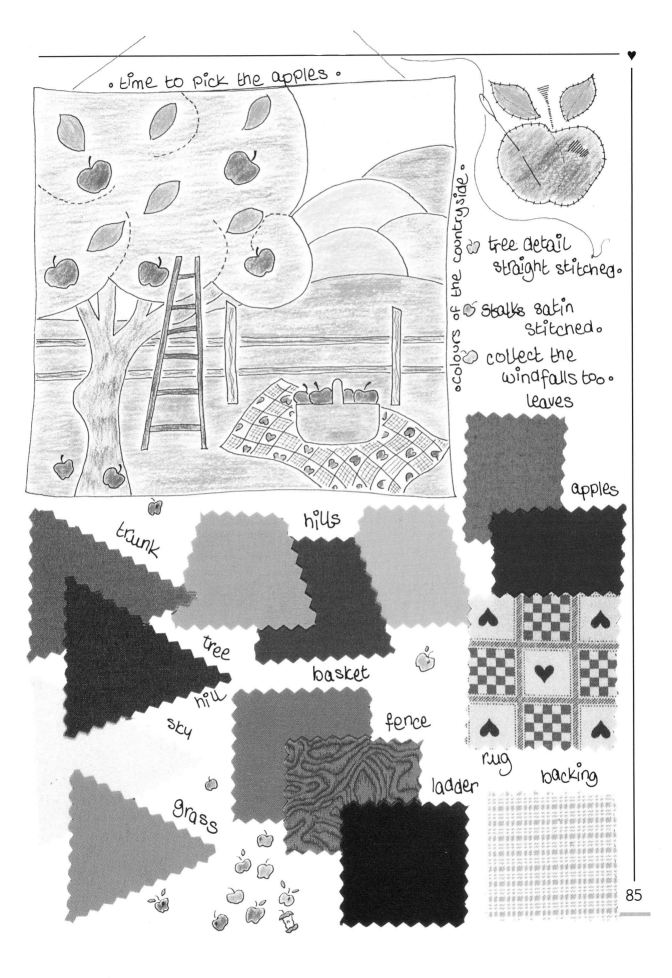

° time to pick the apples °

° colours of the countryside °

tree detail straight stitched °

stalks satin stitched °

collect the windfalls too °

leaves

apples

trunk

hills

tree

basket

hill

sky

fence

rug

ladder

backing

grass

PARTLY PATCHWORK CUSHION

For something completely different try this stunning cushion cover, with its rich, warm, autumn colours offset by a natural ticking (pillow ticking) background, it is sure to provoke comment. Made from four separate squares stitched together to form the front, which is framed with piping made from a combination of the fabrics, it is easy-to-make, although the leaves have lots of points and curves so may be fiddly to stitch.

FINISHED SIZE: *46cm (18in) square*

♥ 50cm (½yd) medium-weight cotton, 115cm (45in) wide, for base/background and backing
♥ Nine 10cm (4in) lengths applique fabric, 115cm (45in) wide, for patchwork, leaves and piping
♥ Threads to match the appliqué fabrics
♥ 2.5m (2½yd) piping cord
♥ 46cm (18in) square cushion pad

1 Prepare your fabrics as described in Pre-stitching Preparation (page 17), although the fabrics that are to be used for the patchwork strips do not have vilene (pellon) on the back.

2 The cushion top is made from four 24cm (9½in) squares, which, after stitching together, give a finished size 46cm (18in) square. Cut two 24cm (9½in) squares of the base/background fabric ready for the appliqué. Tack (baste) a 23cm (9in) square onto each one, appliqué within them.

3 From the selected fabrics cut fifteen strips each 4cm (1½in) wide (this includes a 6mm (¼in) seam allowance down each side) by 38cm (15in) long, for each patchwork square. As the patchwork is used diagonally, the completed square has to be larger than needed, then cut to

°the strips of fabric are joined lengthways. seams pressed open.

size. Using 6mm (¼in) seams, join all the strips together lengthways, in whichever order you choose. Press open the seams (see drawing below).
From this pieced square and with the strips diagonal, cut a 24cm (9½in) square. Repeat the whole process for the second pieced square.

4 Cut out all the appliqué shapes using the templates on page 112. Tack (baste) then satin stitch the leaves onto the two base/background squares, except for one small one which will overlap the patchwork. Add the vein details and stalks using satin stitch (see worksheet right).

5 With right sides facing, stitch together one patchwork square and one appliquéd square with a 12mm (½in) seam. Repeat with the two remaining squares, making sure they are the opposite way round to the first two (see worksheet right). Press open the seams. Stitch the two halves of the work together, carefully matching the centre seams and making sure that the two appliquéd squares are diagonally opposite each other (see worksheet). Press open the seam.

6 Appliqué the last small leaf in place just over the centre seam. The cushion front is now complete.

7 Piece the fabric for the piping using the method described in Finishing (page 26). Cover the piping cord and attach to the cushion as described in Finishing (page 26).

8 Cut out the back and complete the cushion as described in Finishing (page 27).

satin & straight stitch detail onto leaves ✿ piping fabric is pieced ✿
patchwork strips are randomly arranged in an order pleasing to you ✿

draw inspiration from the burning autumn colours ✿

the leaves creating a patchwork where they fall ✿

°such richness°
1° 2° 3°
base/ background
4° 5° 6°
°all fabrics, except base, are in the patchwork °

SUNNY WINDOW
WALLHANGING

A scene from a hot summer day is the inspiration for this striking, easy to complete design. A cat contrasts with a pot of geraniums, both offset by the reflection of the sky in the window. The geranium is simplified in form with two leaves made as completely separate pieces, then stitched in place when the appliqué is finished.

FINISHED SIZE: 40.5 × 51cm (16 × 20in)

♥   50cm (½yd) lightweight calico (muslin), 115cm (45in) wide, for the base and backing
♥   50cm (½yd) square lightweight cotton, for the background
♥   25cm (¼yd) appliqué fabric, 115cm (45in) wide, for the window frames and loops
♥   Four 10cm (4in) lengths appliqué fabric, 115cm (45in) wide, for the window ledge, wall, curtains, leaves and stems
♥   Scraps of appliqué fabric, for the flowers and flower pot
♥   30cm (12in) square appliqué fabric, for cat
♥   Threads to match the appliqué fabrics
♥   Rod and cord for hanging

1   Prepare your fabrics as described in Pre-stitching Preparation (page 17).

2   Cut a piece of calico (muslin) 43 × 53.5cm (17 × 21in), including a 12mm (½in) seam allowance all round. For the bordering window frames, cut three lengths of fabric 3cm (1¼in) wide, two 39cm (15¼in) long, one 44cm (17½in) long. Cut a bottom window frame 4cm (1½in) wide × 44cm (17½in). For the narrow glazing bars cut two lengths 12mm (½in) wide × 38cm (15in), then cut one length in half. Cut a window ledge strip 6cm (2¼in) wide x 44cm (17½in), and a wall strip 6.5cm (2½in) wide x 44cm (17½in).

3   Cut out all the appliqué shapes using the templates on page 116. Draw the the curtains and stems, on the back of the fabric freehand, cut out. To make the two separate leaves see step 8.

4   Tack (baste) the background fabric over the base fabric. The curtains are satin stitched onto the base/background fabric first, except for the areas to be overlapped. Refer to Stitching Techniques (page 22). Apply the window: the narrow glazing bars first, then the wide side frames then the top and bottom frames (see worksheet right).

5   Satin stitch the window ledge in position, then the wall fabric. The stone detail of the wall is machine straight stitches (see worksheet right).

6   Tack (baste) the flower pot and geranium stems in place, then satin stitch, except for the areas overlapped by the cat and leaves. Remove the tacking (basting) from the flower pot when appliqué is complete, to ensure the shape remains flat.

7   Appliqué the flowers, leaves at top of flower pot and the cat. Straight stitch the cat's whiskers.

8   To make the two separate leaves, with wrong sides facing, tack (baste) two pieces of the prepared leaf fabric together. Using the leaf template, draw two outlines onto the fabric. Satin stitch along the outlines, using a close, wide stitch. Cut away the excess fabric, as close to the stitches as possible without snipping them. Attach each leaf onto the work with a couple of hand stitches, they will sit slightly away from the background.

9   Follow the procedure described in Finishing (page 24) to cut out and complete the loops and backing. Thread the rod through the loops and attach the cord.

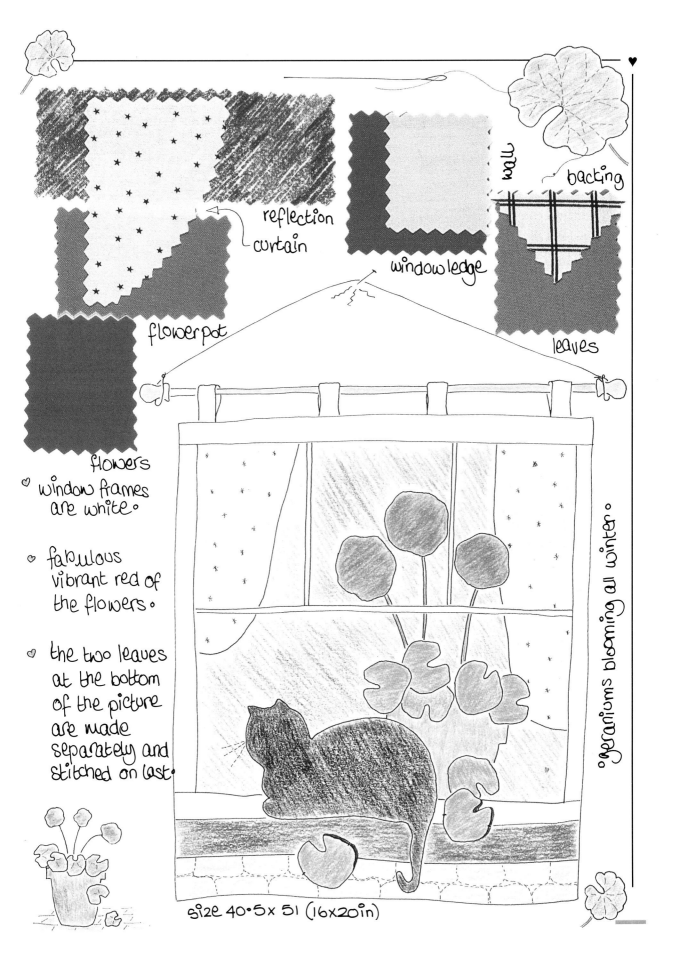

reflection

curtain

window ledge

wall

backing

leaves

flowerpot

flowers

♡ window frames are white.

♡ fabulous vibrant red of the flowers.

♡ the two leaves at the bottom of the picture are made separately and stitched on last.

° geraniums blooming all winter °

size 40·5 x 51 (16x20in)

GLORIOUS RAINBOW
WALLHANGING

The transient, elusive rainbow is one of nature's most wonderful gifts, treasured when seen, but too quickly gone. Stitched onto fabric, however, the image will remain forever. This wallhanging radiates a special warmth and will make any room glow with colour – especially welcome on dreary days. Although the wallhanging is not difficult to make, accurate machining is required when applying the rainbow strips.

FINISHED SIZE: 36 × 44cm (14 × 17¼in)

♥ 50cm (½yd), medium-weight calico (muslin), 137cm (54in) wide, for the base fabric

♥ 50cm (½yd) appliqué fabric, 115cm (45in) wide, for the sky

♥ 25cm (¼yd) appliqué fabric, 115cm (45in) wide, for the curtains and pelmet

♥ Scrap of appliqué fabric for the two tie-backs

♥ Seven 25cm (¼yd) lengths appliqué fabric, 115cm (45in) wide, for the rainbow

♥ Three 36 x 8cm (14 × 3in) strips appliqué fabric, for the fields

♥ 25cm (10in) square appliqué fabric, for the cat

♥ 40 × 8cm (15½ × 3in) strip appliqué fabric, for the windowsill

♥ 50cm (½yd) fabric, 115cm (45in) wide, for the backing and casing

♥ Threads to match the appliqué fabrics

♥ Rod and cord for hanging

1 Cut a piece of the base fabric 37 × 45cm (14½ × 17¾in).

2 Prepare your fabrics as described in Pre-stitching Preparation (page 17).

3 Create the base for the appliqué by covering the calico (muslin) with the prepared sky fabric, tack (baste) together.

4 Cut out the appliqué shapes using the templates on page 117. Draw the fields freehand, on the back of the fabrics, cut out. Adapt the pelmet from the Summer View wallhanging template on page 99.

5 Apply the rainbow first, starting with the red strip. Tack in place then satin stitch along the top edge only. Position the orange strip, slightly overlapping the red by 3mm (⅛in), satin stitch in place along its top edge, securing the bottom edge of the red at the same time. Continue to build up the rainbow in this way. The last strip (purple) is satin stitched along its top and bottom curves.

6 Position the hilly field over the base of the rainbow. Satin stitch in place, except for the areas to be overlapped. Refer to Stitching Techniques (page 22). Apply the remaining two fields, then the windowsill.

7 Apply the cat, then the curtains, tie-backs and finally the pelmet, covering the raw edges at the top of the rainbow.

8 Follow the procedure described in Finishing (page 24) to cut out and complete the backing and casing.

9 Thread the rod through the casing and attach the cord.

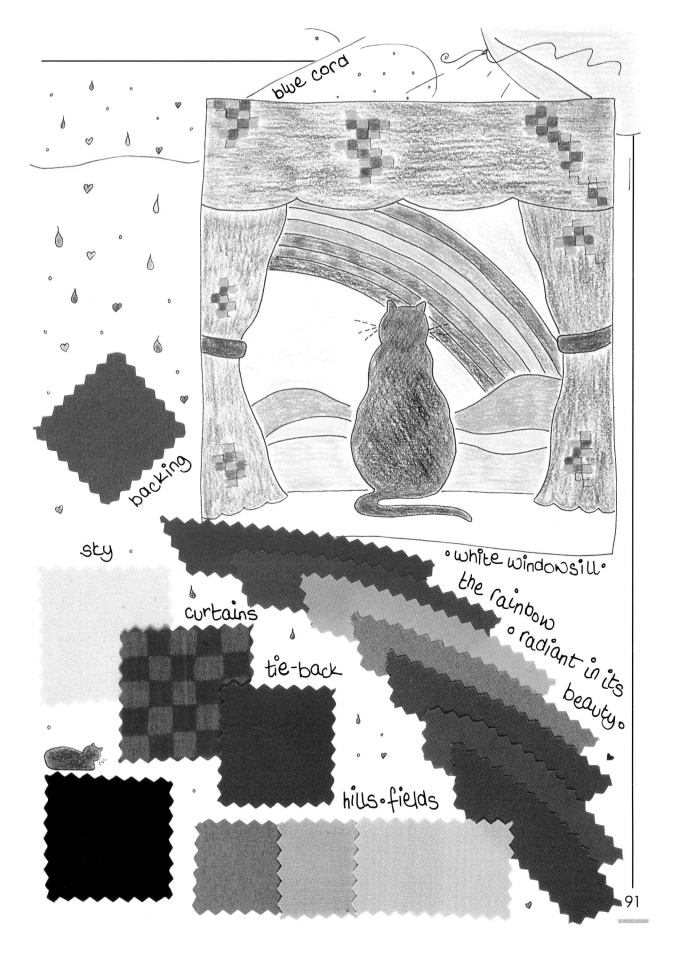

blue cord

backing

sky

curtains

tie-back

white windowsill

the rainbow radiant in its beauty

hills·fields

PROJECT TEMPLATES

NOTE all templates must be enlarged by 120% if using a photocopier (ie, enlarged by 20%) before use in the projects. Any further size alterations necessary are given in the project instructions or on the templates.

To prepare these templates for use either photocopy the relevant page, enlarge the copy as instructed, then trace the shapes individually from this enlarged copy and cut them out; or trace each shape and enlarge by hand before cutting out and using.

No allowances have been made for extra fabric which may be needed for overlapping or underlapping other shapes.

1
HAPPY HEARTS
WALLHANGINGS

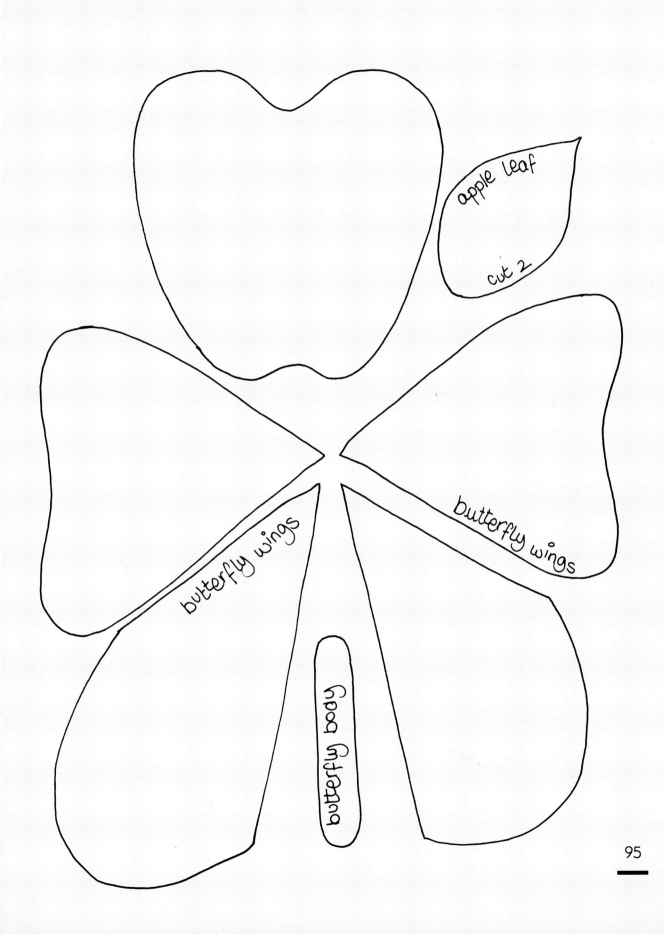

apple leaf

cut 2

butterfly wings

butterfly wings

butterfly body

95

ALPHABETICAL
CUSHIONS

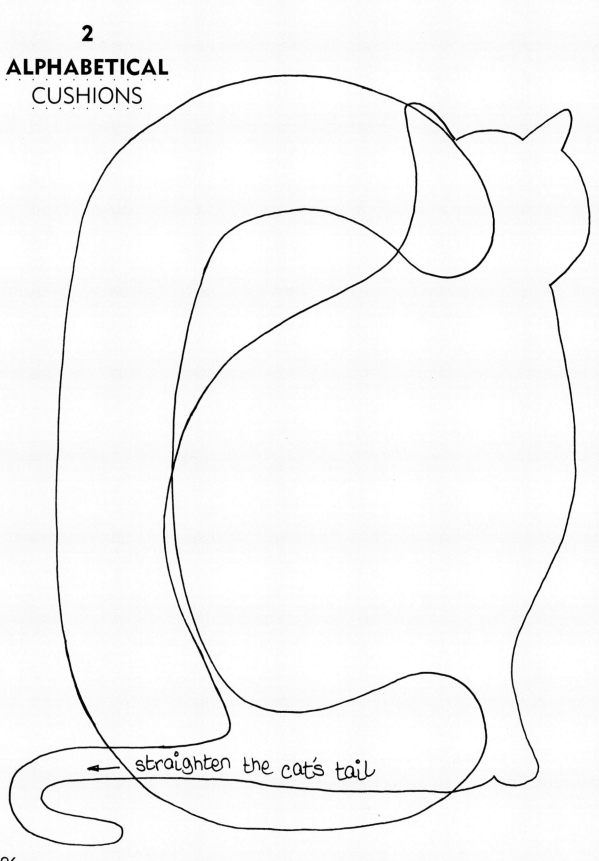

straighten the cat's tail

WALLHANGINGS BY
NUMBERS

cloud

cut 2

tree trunk

flower centre

flower

tree

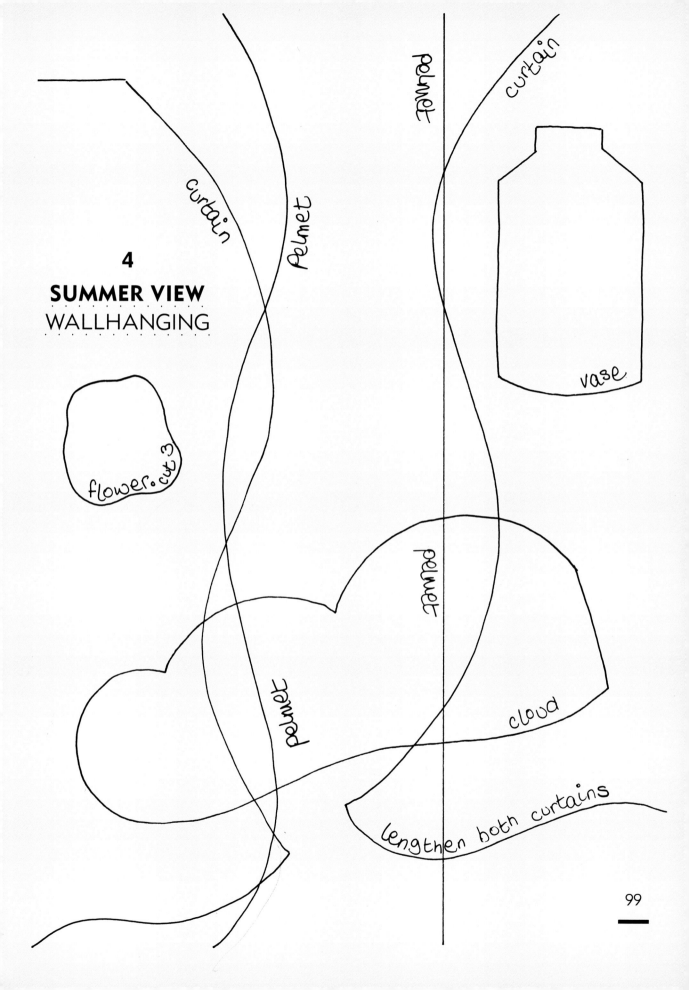

4
SUMMER VIEW
WALLHANGING

curtain

Pelmet

curtain

pelmet

flower. cut 3

vase

pelmet

pelmet

cloud

lengthen both curtains

99

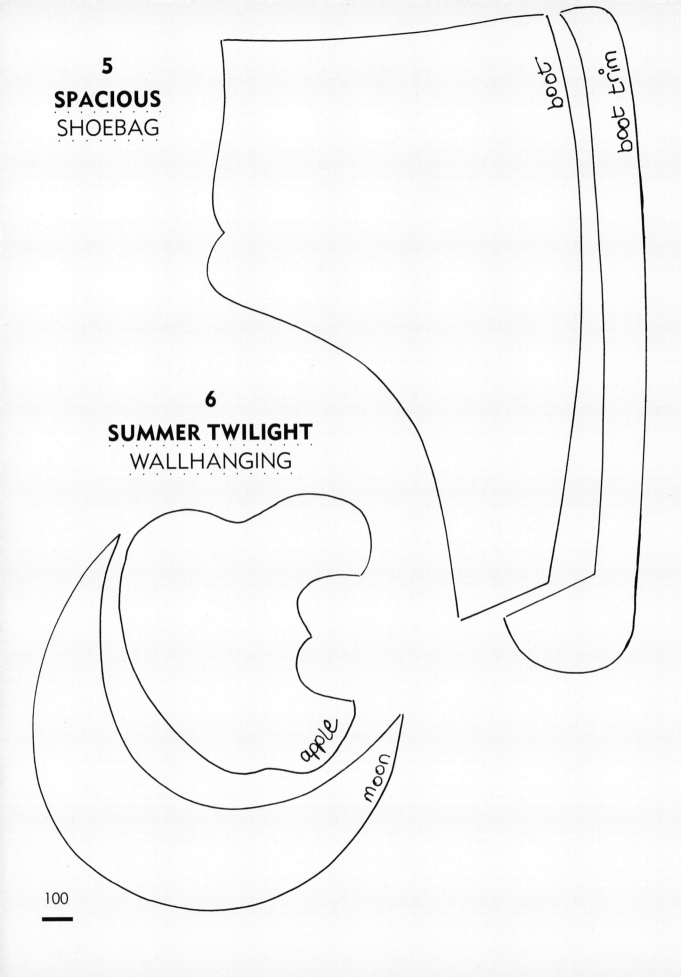

5
SPACIOUS
SHOEBAG

6

SUMMER TWILIGHT
WALLHANGING

boot

boot trim

apple

moon

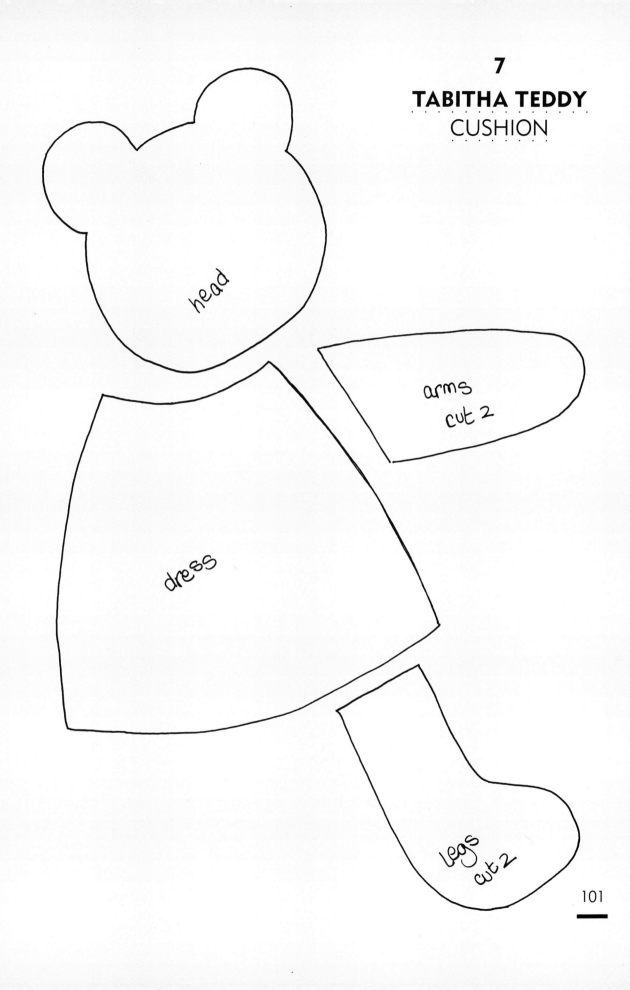

head

arms
cut 2

dress

legs
cut 2

SIMPLY FLORAL
CUSHION

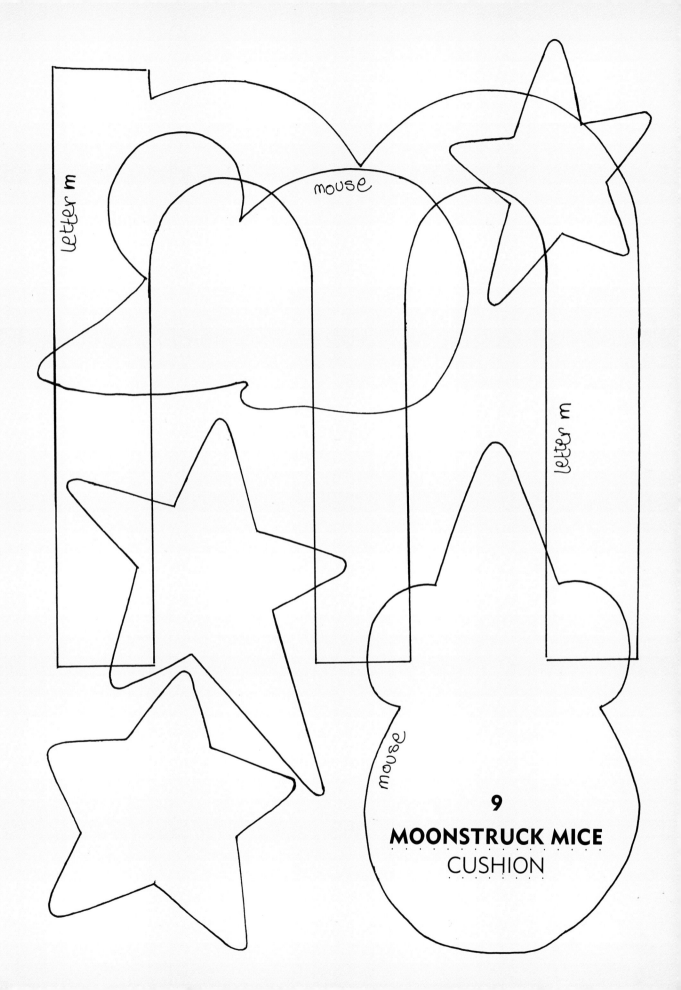

letter m

mouse

letter m

mouse

9
MOONSTRUCK MICE
CUSHION

BAG OF FRUIT

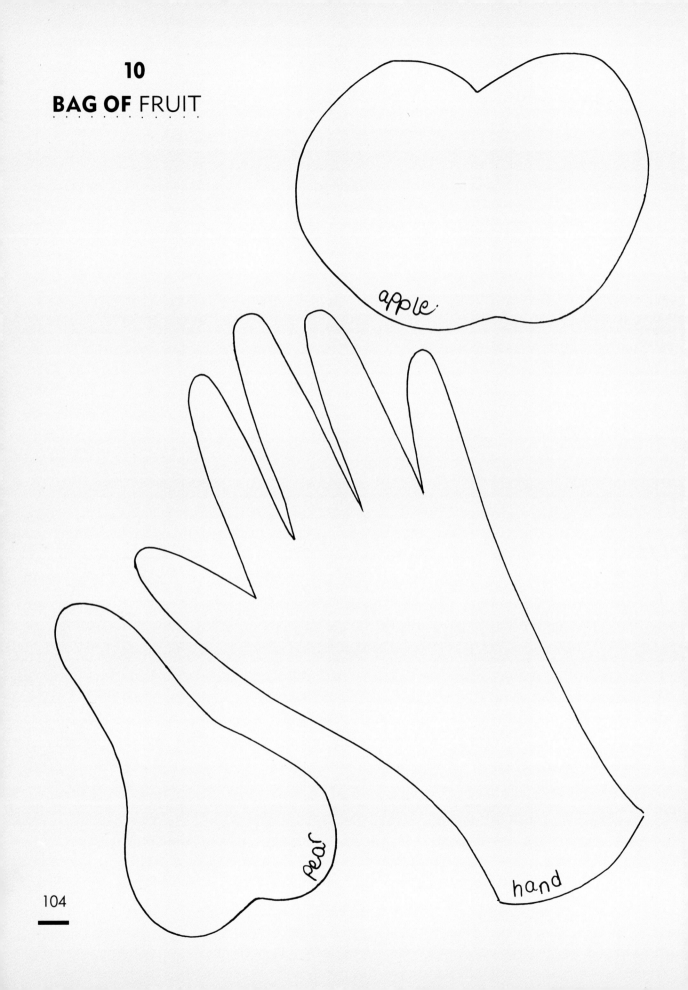

apple

pear

hand

11
SLEEPY TEDDY
COT QUILT

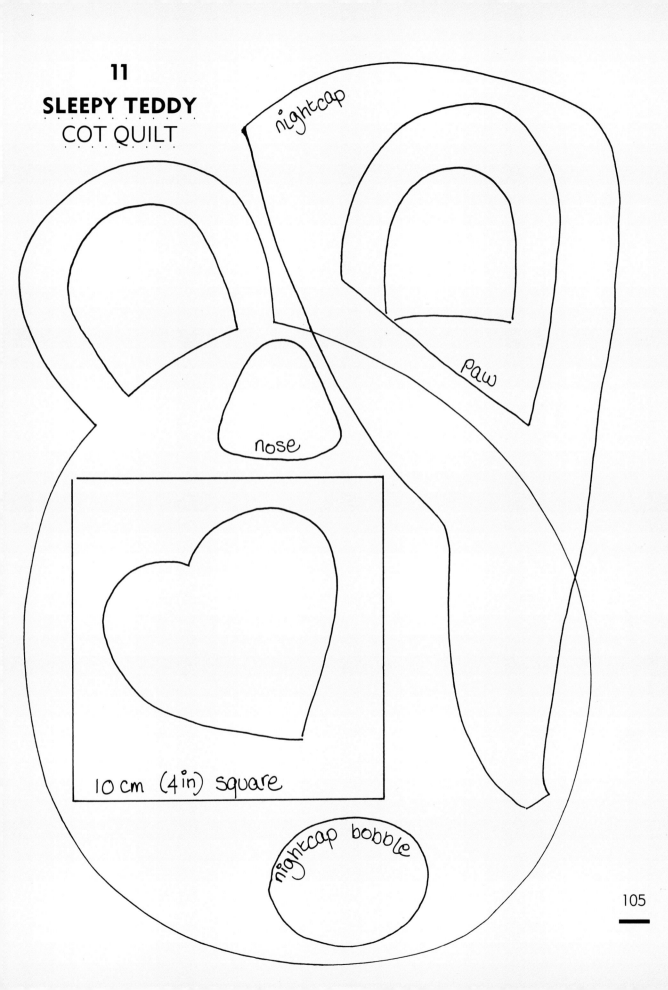

nightcap

paw

nose

10 cm (4in) square

nightcap bobble

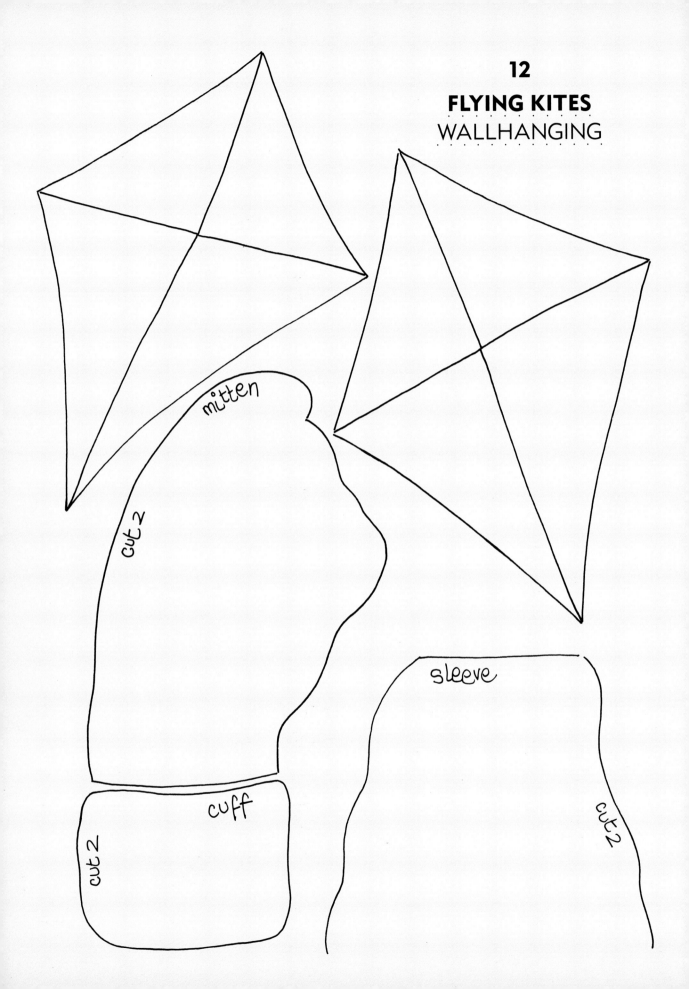

mitten

cut 2

sleeve

cut 2

cuff

cut 2

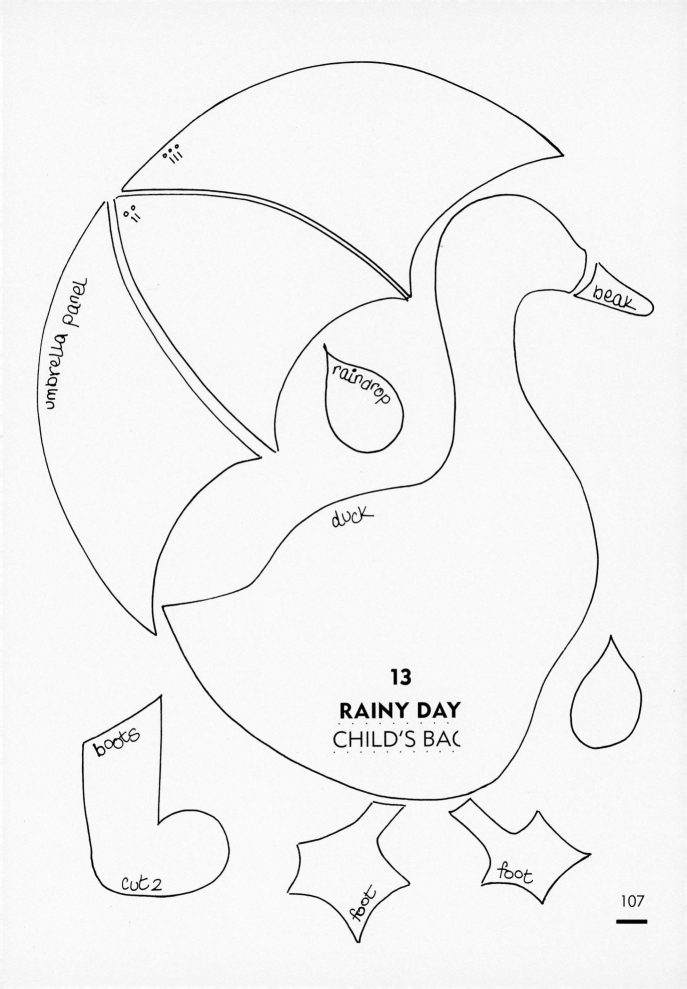

umbrella panel

raindrop

beak

duck

13

RAINY DAY

CHILD'S BAC

boots

cut 2

foot

foot

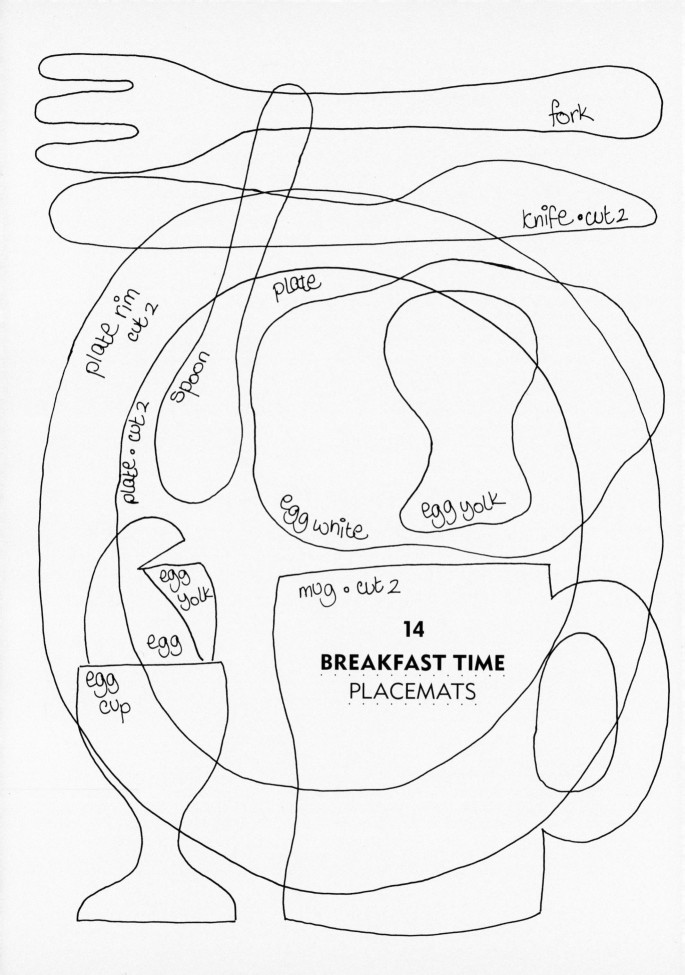

fork

knife • cut 2

plate rim
cut 2

plate

spoon

plate • cut 2

egg white

egg yolk

egg yolk

mug • cut 2

14

BREAKFAST TIME

PLACEMATS

egg

egg cup

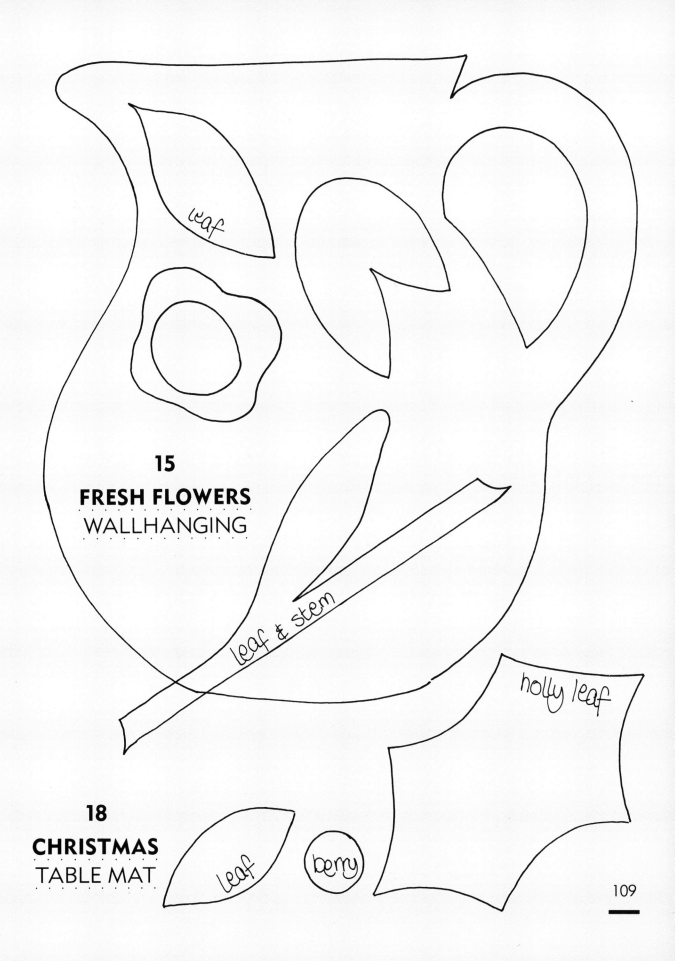

15
FRESH FLOWERS
WALLHANGING

leaf

leaf & stem

18
CHRISTMAS
TABLE MAT

leaf

berry

holly leaf

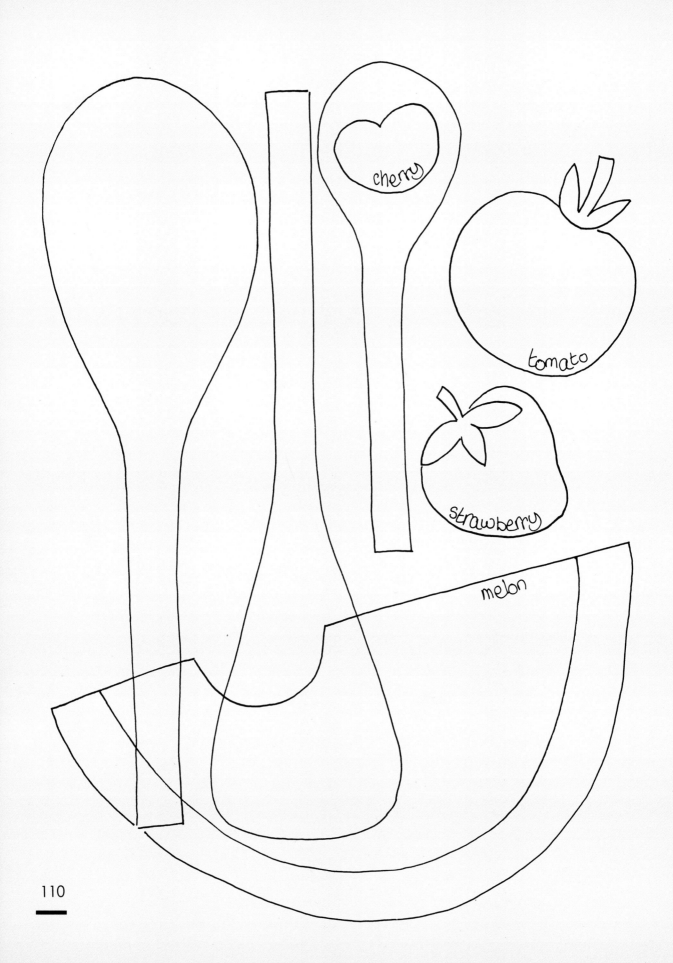

cherry

tomato

strawberry

melon

16

HOME-MADE APRON

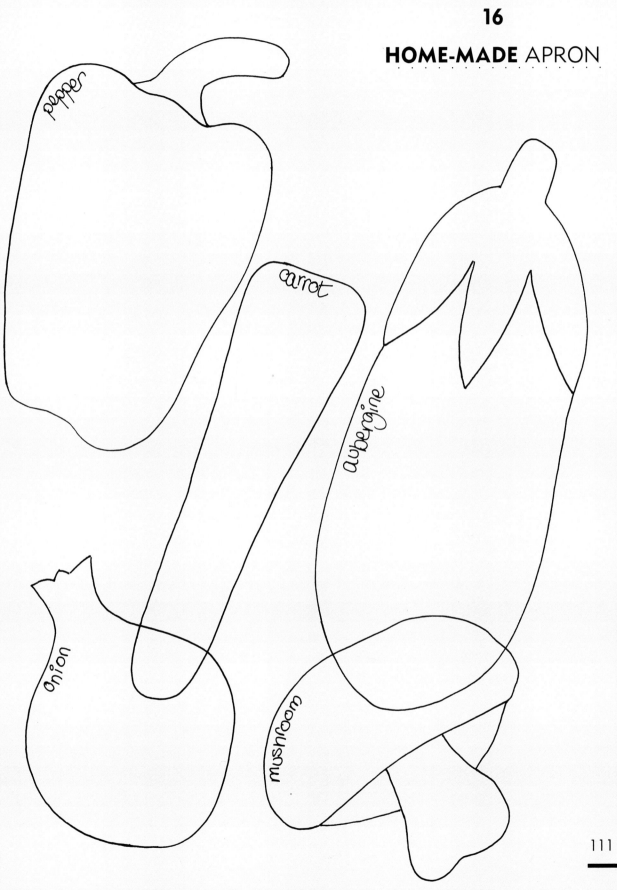

17
SUN, SEA AND SAND BAG

palm leaf cut 3

23
PARTLY PATCHWORK
CUSHION

cut 2

cut 1

cut 2

cut 2

cut 3

cut 5

cut 2

sheep

cut 2

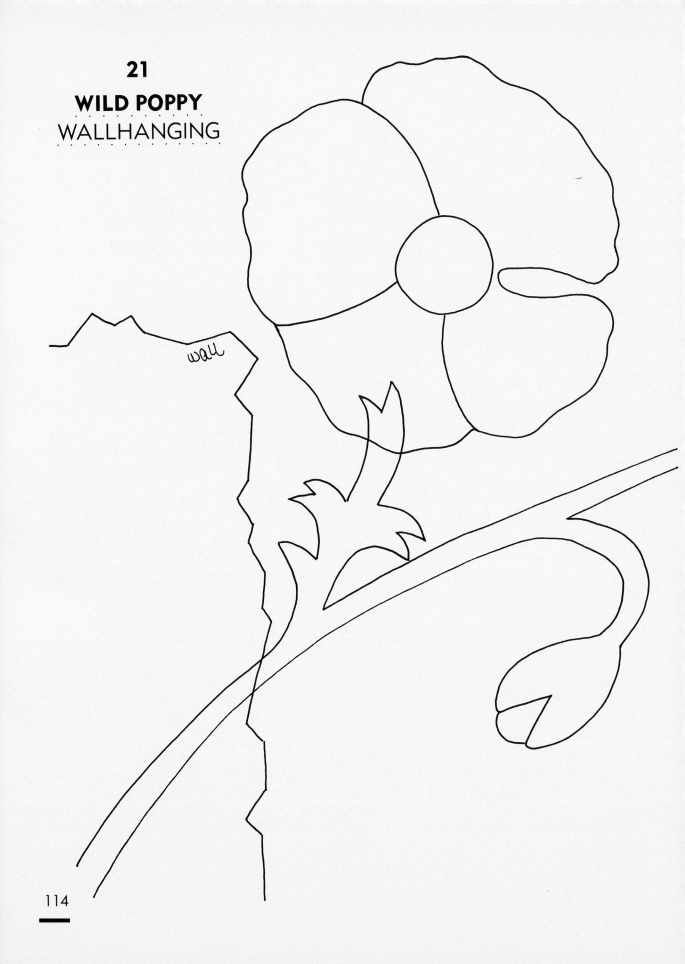

wall

Cut 6

Cut 11

24

SUNNY WINDOW
WALLHANGING

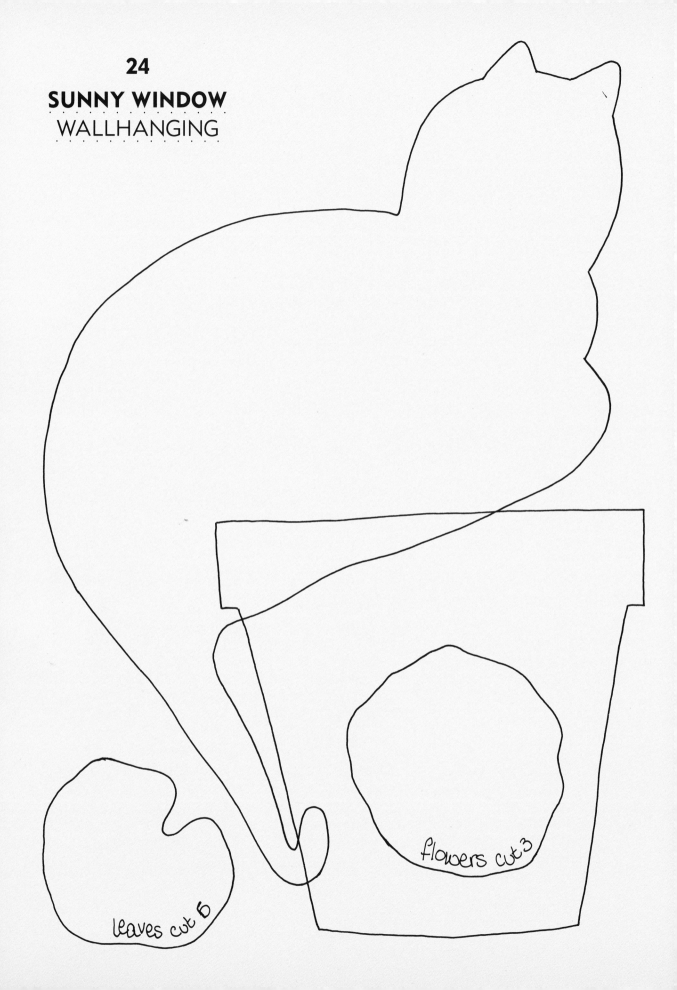

flowers cut 3

leaves cut 6

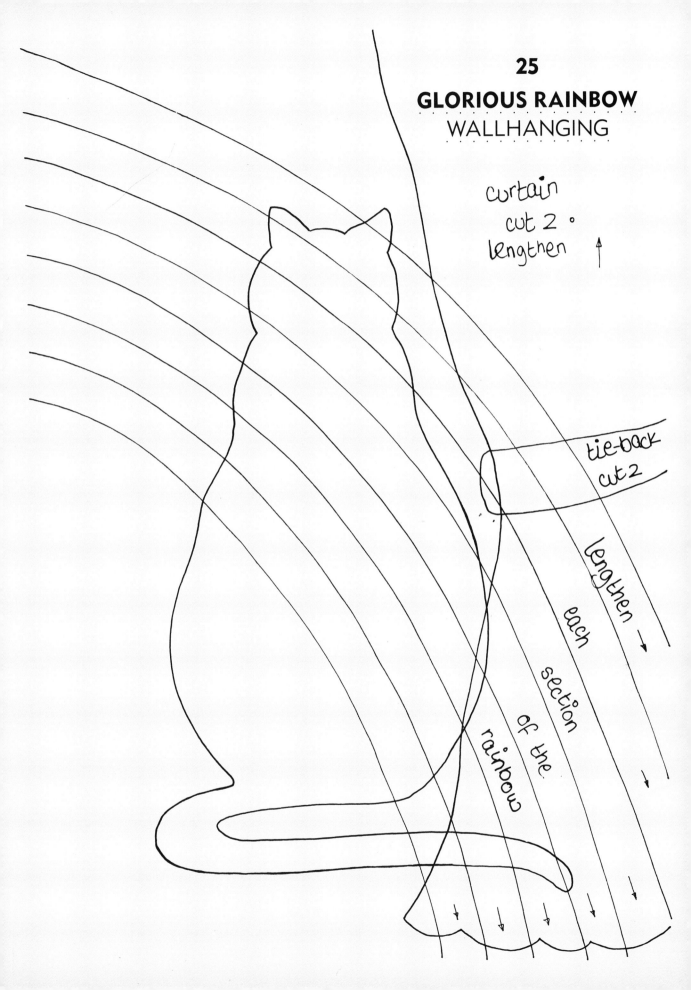

25
GLORIOUS RAINBOW
WALLHANGING

curtain
cut 2 °
lengthen ↑

tie-back
cut 2

lengthen →
each
section
of the
rainbow

USEFUL ADDRESSES

The following list is not intended to be in any way comprehensive. It is always advisable to check opening times before planning any visit.

UNITED KINGDOM

The Quilt Room
20 West Street
Dorking, Surrey RH4 1BL
Tel: 0306 740739
American cotton fabrics.
Shop and mail order.

Strawberry Fayre
Chagford, Newton Abbot,
Devon TQ13 8EN
Tel: 0647 433250
American and English cotton
fabrics.
Mail order only.

Crimple Craft
1 Freemans Way
Wetherby Road
Harrogate, North Yorkshire
HG3 1RW
Tel: 0423 885430
American cotton fabrics.
Shop and mail order.

Village Fabrics
Unit 7, Bushells Business Estate
Wallingford, Oxon OX10 0DD
Tel: 0491 36178
American cotton fabrics.
Shop and mail order

Campden Cotton Club
Island Cottage
High Street
Chipping Campden,
Gloucestershire GL55 6AT
Tel: 0386 840268
All natural fabrics of varying
weights.
Shop.

Campden Quilters Patch
Blacksmiths House
High Street
Chipping Campden,
Gloucestershire GL55 6AT
Tel: 0386 840181
Cotton prints and plains.
Shop, fabrics by post.

Whaleys (Bradford) Ltd
Harris Court
Bradford, West Yorkshire BD7 4EQ
Tel: 0274 576718
All types of basic fabrics.
Fabrics by post.

Ian Mankin
109 Regents Park Road
Primrose Hill, London NW1 8UR
Tel: 071 722 0997
Natural fabrics for curtains and
upholstery. Tickings, ginghams,
stripes, plains, tartans and more.
Shop, fabrics by post.

C A Wilkinson
16-18 Sidney Street
Sheffield S1 4RN
Tel: 0742 755698
Hand ground and crafted scissors.

Calico Basket
6A Main Street
Hillsborough
Co Down, Northern Ireland
BT26 6AE
Tel: 0846 682863
American cotton fabrics.
Shop, fabrics by post.

Abakhan Fabrics
Llanerch-y-mor
Mostyn, Nr Holywell
Clwyd, Wales CH8 9DX
Tel: 0745 560312
American and English cotton
fabrics.
Shop, fabrics by post.

The Hobby Shop
Main Street
Alford
Aberdeenshire, Scotland
AB33 8TX
Tel: 09755 62963
American and English cotton
fabrics.
Shop, fabrics by post.

UNITED STATES

Most fabric stores in America sell cotton fabrics, and there are many quilter's supply stores. For further information refer to magazines such as Quilter's Newsletter and Quiltmaker.

Quilts and Other Comforts
PO Box 394-226
Wheatridge, CO 80034-0394

Gutcheon Patchworks
11002 Valley Avenue East
Puyallup, WA 98372

Great Expectations
14520 Memorial Drive #54
Houston, TX 77089

Glad Creations
3400 Bloomington Avenue South
Minneapolis, MN 55407

Empty Spools
70 Bradley
Walnut Creek, CA 94596

Strawberry Patch
Columbia Crossroads, PA 16914

Hancock Fabrics
3841 Hinterville Road,
Interstate #24
Paducah, KY 42001

AUSTRALIA

Refer to Down Under Quilts *or* Australian Country Craft *magazines, both of which have stockists of cotton fabrics listed in them.*

The Calico Patch
O'Hanlon Place
Gungahlin 2912, Capital Territory

Anne's Glory Box
60-62 Beaumont Street
Hamilton 2303, New South Wales

Alice Traders
2 Schwartz Crescent
Alice Springs 0870,
Northern Territory

Krafty Kats
Shop 14, Robina Shopping Village
Robina 4226, Queensland

Barossa Quilt & Craft Cottage
Angaston Road
Nurioopta 5355, South Australia

American Patchworks
91 Patrick Street
Hobart 7000, Tasmania

Patchwork Plus
464 High Street
East Kew 3102, Victoria

Calico House
2 Napoleon Street
Cottesloe 6011, Western Australia

NEW ZEALAND

Canvas Craft
PO Box 825
Blenheim

Jan's Patch
235 Moray Place
Dunedin

Karori Wool & Patchwork
148 Karori Road
Wellington

Sewing Box
Courtville Place
101 Dee Street
Invercargill

ACKNOWLEDGEMENTS

For Juliet. My guide in my quest for the truth.

Abi, Tom and Hannah, who have lived with me during the gestation period of my book and endured a surfeit of fabric and a distracted mother, deserve my special love and gratitude. My heartfelt thanks to Alison, who has helped me with some of the stitching and listened to my ideas and endless ponderings; to Carole, Phil, Leslie and David, for their unwavering encouragement; to Vivienne, the editor at David & Charles, for guiding this new author through her first book with patience, clarity and support. I also thank Pam and Jayne who, always cheerful and uncomplaining, have waded their way through my longhand and converted it into the typewritten manuscript, and Dave who made the final delivery to Newton Abbot. Finally in appreciation of the work undertaken at David & Charles by those people who transform my work, magically, into a book.

INDEX

Page numbers in *italic* indicate illustrations